MASTERY
PRACTICE BOOK
Learn to apply knowledge and
get higher grades.

Created by Dr Tony Sherborne, with the Mastery Science team:
Gemma Young, Helen Harden, Jude Sanders

Teacher writers: Gemma Young, Robin Young, Kat Day, Helen Dixon,
Ruth Smith, Ursilla Brown, Ian Horsewell, Alison Dennis

Design by: Alexandra Okada & Stuart Norwood

mastery science

Contents

How to use the book

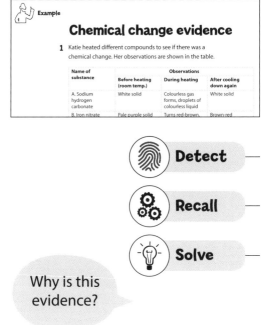

Detect

Recall

Solve

Why is this evidence?

Your turn

| 1 | /3 | 2 | /3 | 3 | /3 |

Hints & Answers

Watch out !

Mixed up problems

Applying what you know is not easy. Keep trying, and learn from your mistakes. With practice you will master the concepts and be confident with whatever examiners ask.

The *Example* pages have 3 steps:

Work out what you need to do to answer the question.

Bring to mind what you already know about the concept. Showing it visually helps the thinking process.

Go from what you know to the answer, step-by-step.

Do answer the questions in speech bubbles. This will help you follow the example and remember the main points.

The *Your Turn* pages have three practice questions. The first is very similar to the example. Look back and copy the steps. The other two questions might look different but they are testing the same thinking process.

Use the scoring box to check how you're doing. Award yourself 3 points if you did Detect, Recall and Solve well. Subtract 1 point for each step you didn't do well. +1 if you answered without a hint.

If you're stuck, go to the *Hints* pages at the back. The hint is a clue or question to get you moving. Use the *Answers* pages to check if you were correct. If you weren't, look back at the example and figure out what you did wrong.

The *Watch Out* pages are to help you avoid common mistakes and clear up confusions in your knowledge.

Now you're ready for the challenge at the end of the chapter: *Mixed up problems.* This is like an exam where different types of questions are jumbled up. Don't panic, just follow the 3 steps: Detect, Recall and Solve. If you get stuck, look back at the example or try a hint.

Good luck!

1.1 Find missing force

1 A car travels at constant speed. The diagram shows the forces on the car.

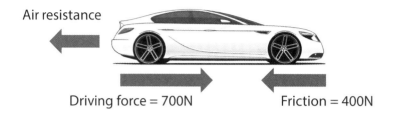

Air resistance

Driving force = 700N   Friction = 400N

Calculate the force of air resistance.

 Detect

I know all the forces on the car except one. I have to calculate the missing force.

Recall

Constant speed (or at rest) means the forces are balanced. So,
Sum of forces in one direction = Sum of force in opposite direction.

Why is this equation true?

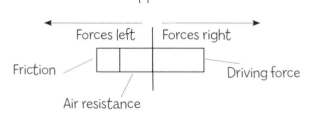

Forces left | Forces right

Friction

Air resistance

Driving force

Solve

Put the values from the question into the balanced forces diagram:

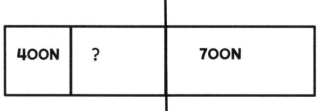

| 400N | ? | 700N |

How did I work this out?

We can write this as an equation:

400N + air resistance = 700 N

So, air resistance = 700- 400

= 300 N

2 The hot air balloon is climbing at a steady speed. Calculate the air resistance.

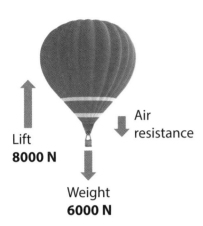

Lift
8000 N

Air resistance

Weight
6000 N

3 Two boys pull and push a box with the same force. The box moves at a steady speed. Calculate the push and pull force.

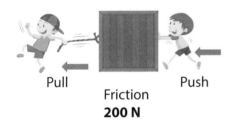

Pull

Friction
200 N

Push

4 The weight is supported by the tension in two identical springs. What is the tension in each spring?

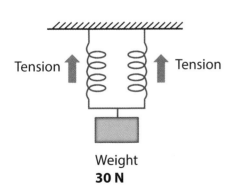

Tension

Tension

Weight
30 N

1.2 Explain floating & sinking

1 An empty plastic cup has a mass of 20g and volume of 100 cm³.
The diagram shows how it floats in water.

How much water do you need to add to make the cup sink?
The density of water is 1g/cm³.

 Detect

I need to work out how the density of the cup compares to that of water.

 Recall

How does the cup's density compare to 1g/cm3?

Density much lower than water's

Density nearly as big as water's

1. An object floats when its density is smaller than the density of the fluid (e.g. water).
2. An object's density is its mass/its volume.
3. The density of water is 1g/cm³, so 1g of water has a volume of 1 cm³.
4. The closer the object's density is to the fluid's, the more of it floats below the surface.
5. If the density equals the fluid's, the object floats with all its volume below.
6. If its density is bigger than the fluid's, the object sinks.

 Solve

The empty cup's density is its mass/its volume
= 20 g/100 cm³
= 0.2 g/cm³

Adding water increases the cup's mass but not its volume. So its density increases and it floats lower in the water.

When the density of cup + water = 1 g/ cm³, the whole cup will be under the water (and about to sink).

That means the mass of cup + water needs to be 100 g.
(because 100 g/100 cm³ = 1 cm³)

Why is the mass 100g when it's about to sink?

As the empty cup is 20 g, we need to add just a little more than 80 g of water to make it sink.

Your turn

2 A ship carrying steel poles floats on a lake. The poles are thrown overboard and sink.
Does the boat float higher or lower in the water?
Explain your answer.

Material	Density (g/cm³)
Teak	0.98
Water	1.00
Cooking oil	0.90
Mercury	13.60

3 A block of teak wood is placed in a glass of water. It floats on the surface.

Use the information in the table to explain what will happen to the teak when it is put into:
i) Cooking oil
ii) Mercury.

4 Jay blows a little air into a balloon. She puts it into a sealed jar. The balloon sinks to the bottom.
She then fills the balloon with helium. It rises to the top.

What would happen to the balloon if Jay filled the jar with helium instead of air? Explain your answer.

Example

1.3 Calculate density

1 Sami wins a gold trophy. He wants to know if it's pure or if the gold is mixed with a cheaper metal.

The trophy has a volume of 100 cm³ and a mass of 1500 g. Gold has a density of 19 g/cm³.

Explain whether you think the trophy is pure gold or not.

 Detect

We need to calculate the density of the trophy and compare it to that of gold.

 Recall

What does the property of a material mean?

1cm³ of gold = 19 g

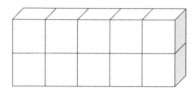

10 1cm³ cubes = 190 g

1. Density is a property of a material. Gold has a very large density, 19 g/cm³ . Most metals are much less dense.
2. Density means how much mass a cube 1 cm x 1 cm x 1 cm has.
3. 10 cubes or 10 cm³ of gold has a mass of 10 x 19 = 190 g.
4. The formula to calculate density is: density = $\frac{mass}{volume}$

 Solve

Why does the other metal change the trophy's density?

Method 1: Work out the mass of 100 cm³ of gold (the volume of Sami's trophy).

100 cubes or 100 cm³ of gold has a mass of 100x 19 =1900 g.
But the material in Sami's trophy has a mass of 1500 g for 100 cm³ - much less than if it were pure gold So the gold must be mixed with another metal.

You can imagine that some of the non-gold cubes in Sami's trophy have a lower mass, giving it a lower density.

Method 2: Calculate the density of Sami's trophy.
density = $\frac{mass}{volume}$ = $\frac{1500 \text{ g}}{100 \text{ g}}$ = 15 g/cm³

This material of Sami's trophy has a lower density than gold, so it cannot be pure gold.

Your turn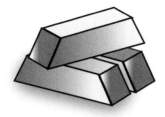

2

Alexa has three materials with the properties below.

A   Mass 40 g   Volume 5 cm³

B   Mass 40 g   Volume 10 cm³

C   Mass 20 g   Volume 10 cm³

Which material is the most dense? Explain your answer.

3 Kyle has a block of wood. It has a volume of 100 cm³. She knows it has a mass of 1800 g.
What is the density of the block?

A   18 g/cm³   **B**   5 g/cm³   **C**   1.8 g/cm³   **D**   0.05 g/cm³

4

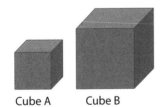

Cube A   Cube B

Both these cubes have the same mass but different volumes.
Which cube has a bigger density? Explain your choice.

| 1 | /3 | 2 | /3 | 3 | /3 | no hints: +1 Total | /10 | 9 |

1.4 Friction factors

1 Pablo investigated the force needed to pull weights along different surfaces.

i) Predict the results he got by putting the missing values into the table.

ii) Which surface creates more friction? Give a reason.

Weight (N)	Force needed Surface 1 (N)	Force needed Surface 2 (N)
1	0.8	0.5
2		
4		
8		

Detect

I need to work out how the weight affects the force of friction.

Recall

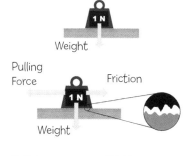

Weight

Pulling Force — Friction

Weight

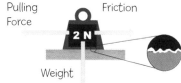

Pulling Force — Friction

Weight

Why does a rough surface cause more friction?

1. Gravity pulls the weight down on to the table surface. The bigger the weight, the more it presses the surfaces against each other.

2. The surfaces stick together a bit. This causes friction. The rougher the surfaces, the more they stick.

3. The bigger the weight, the more stick there is and the greater the friction.

4. To move the block, the pull has to be bigger than the force of friction.

5. When the weight is bigger, it takes a bigger force to overcome the greater friction.

Solve

Why does the force double each time?

i)

Weight doubles between each reading

Weight pulled (N)	Force needed Surface 1 (N)	Force needed Surface 2 (N)
1	0.8	0.5
2	1.6	1.0
4	3.2	2.0
8	6.4	4.0

Friction doubles between each reading

ii) From the table, surface 1 needs a greater pulling force for every weight. So it must create more friction. This is because the rougher the surface, the more the weight "sticks".

Hint p.127, Answers p.130

2 Christina wants to find out the force needed to pull weights on a rough surface.

i) Predict her results by filling in the table with the missing values for weights.

Weight being pulled (N)	Force needed (N)
1	1.2
	2.4
	3.6
	4.8

ii) Explain how you worked out the missing values.

3 Which graph shows the relationship between the weight of an object and the frictional force? Explain your choice.

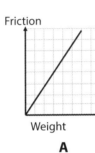

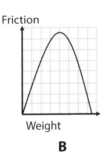

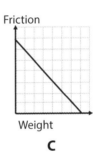

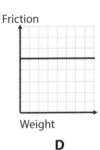

A   B   C   D

4 Dalia measured the friction for different shoes in her family. The table shows her results.

Shoe size	Shoe type	Friction (N)
Size 3	Slippers	3.2
Size 6	Trainers	4.2
Size 9	Walking boots	4.6

She concluded that friction increases with shoe size because bigger shoes have a larger surface area.

Describe a different explanation for the pattern.

| 1 | /3 | 2 | /3 | 3 | /3 | no hints: +1 Total | /10 |

11

1.5 Friction and motion

1 A racing driver measured how the speed of his car changed.

i) The car took only 6.7 seconds to go from 0-100 mph. It took 20 seconds to go from 100-200 mph. Why did it take longer to go from 100-200 mph?

ii) The car would not go faster than 233 mph. Why did it reach a top speed?

 Detect

I need to think about net force and how it changes at different speeds.

Recall

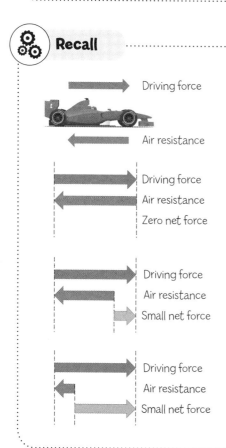

In which direction is the net force?

1. The forces on the car are its driving force and air resistance.

2. The faster the car goes, the bigger the air resistance.

3. When the driving force and air resistance are equal, the net force is zero. The car travels at constant speed.

4. When the driving force is a little bigger than air resistance, there is a small net force. The car speeds up slowly.

5. When the driving force is much bigger than air resistance, there is a large net force. The car speeds up quickly.

 Solve

Which sentence explains top speed?

i) From 0-100 mph: the air resistance is small, the net force is big and the car speeds up quickly.

From 100-200 mph: the air resistance is large, the net force is small and the car speeds up slowly.

ii) At 233 mph:, air resistance is so high that it equals the driving force. So the net force is zero and the car does not speed up any more.

Your turn

2 Sharmilla pedals with a constant force. The table shows how long it takes her to reach 20 mph, and then 25 mph.

Use the idea of forces to explain why:
i) She speeds up more in the first 10 seconds
ii) She cannot go faster than 25 mph.

Speed (mph)	Increase in speed (mph)	Time (s)
10-20	10	10
20-25	5	10

3 Niall drops a metal ball into a cylinder containing oil. He marks the position of the ball every second and calculates the speed. The table shows his results.

i) Describe how the speed changes over 5 seconds
ii) Explain this pattern in terms of drag and weight.

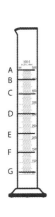

Time (s)	Mark	Speed (cm/s)
0	A	0
1	B	0.5
2	C	0.9
3	D	1.2
4	E	1.4
5	F	1.5

Drag

Weight

4 The graph below shows how the air resistance of a skydiver changes as she falls.

i) Explain why the air resistance increases and reaches a maximum.
ii) Add another line onto the graph to show the weight of the skydiver.

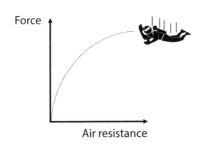

Force

Air resistance

1.6 Mixed up problems

1 The weight of the table is supported by the upward reaction from the floor on each leg. What is the reaction on each leg?

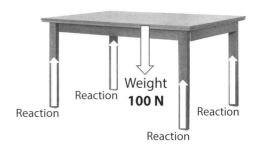

2 The table shows the masses and volumes of different objects. Which object has the highest density?

Object	Mass (g)	Volume (cm³)
A	11	24
B	11	12
C	55	4
D	55	11

3 Alison pours honey, water, alcohol and oil into a test tube. The liquids settles into four layers, one on top of another. The table shows the densities of the liquids.

What is the correct order of the liquid layers, from top to bottom?

Liquid	Density (g/cm³)
Alcohol	0.8
Honey	1.4
Oil	0.9
Water	1.0

A   Honey, water, oil, alcohol

B   Alcohol, honey, oil, water

C   Honey, oil, alcohol, water

D   Alcohol, oil, water, honey.

1   /3   2   /3   3   /3   no hints: +1 Total   /10   © Mastery Science 2017

4 The more an object weighs, the bigger the force of friction stopping it move. The graph shows this relationship for a smooth surface.

How would the line look for a rough surface?

Show this by sketching another line on the same axes.

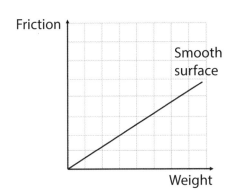

5 A student investigated the friction on her trainer. She wrote:

"I pulled harder and harder until I overcame friction."

Estimate the force of friction from the table.

Explain your answer.

A 2.5 N   **B** 3 N   **C** 2.5 - 3 N

Pull (N)	1	1.5	2	2.5	3
Shoe moves?	No	No	No	No	Yes

6 When a feather is dropped, the forces on it are its weight and drag.

Which graph shows how the drag force on the feather changes:

i) On Earth

ii) On the Moon. Give a reason for your answers.

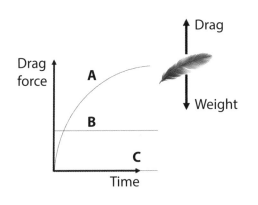

2.1 Complete loops

1 Which switch or switches must be closed so that two bulbs are lit?

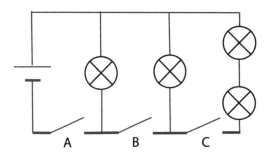

A   B   C

 Detect

I need to work out whether current flows in each loop or not.

When will a bulb light up?

 Recall

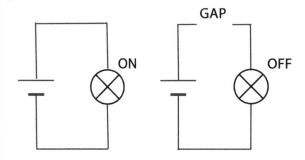

ON   GAP   OFF

1. A bulb only lights if there is a complete loop.
2. Current is a flow of electrons around the circuit.
3. An open switch creates a gap. Electrons stop moving and no current flows.

 Solve

Switch A is part of the loops of every bulb. It must be closed or none of the bulbs will be lit.

Switch B is part of the loops for bulbs 2, 3 and 4. If it is open, only bulb 1 is lit and the rest are off. So switch B must be closed.

How can I make complete loops with two bulbs?

Switch C is only part of the loops for bulbs 3 and 4. If it is open, bulbs 1 and 2 are still lit and bulbs 3 and 4 are off. So when switch C is open two bulbs are lit.

The answer is: switches A and B must be closed, and switch C open.

2

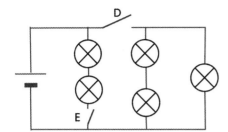

Explain how you can have exactly two bulbs lit in this circuit.

3

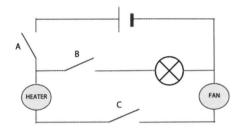

Can you have the heater on and the fan off at the same time? Explain your answer.

4

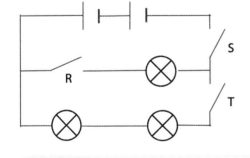

How many bulbs light if switch R is open and switches S and T are closed? Give an explanation.

2.2 Ammeter readings

1 **i)** What current flows through bulb 1?

ii) If bulb 1 breaks, what happens to the readings on each ammeter?

Explain your answers.

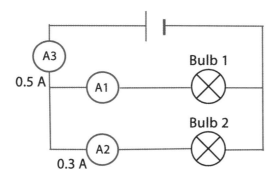

 Detect

I need to work out what happens when a loop splits or joins another.

Why is this true?

 Recall

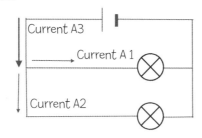

1. Current can only flow in a complete loop.
2. The current is the same all around a loop.
3. Current changes when a loop splits off or joins another loop. Some current goes each way at a split and then it meets up again at a join.
4. The current in loop 3 = the sum of the currents going though the loops 1 and 2:

   current in A3 = current in A1 + current in A2

 Solve

i) We know current in A3 = 0.5 A and current in A2 = 0.3 A
So 0.5 A = current in A1 + 0.3

Changing the subject of the formula to A1:
current in A1 = 0.5 A - 0.3 A = 0.2 A.

ii) If bulb 1 breaks, there is an incomplete loop through A1. So ammeter A1 reads zero.

The loop through bulb 2 is not affected. So ammeter A2 still reads 0.3 A To work out the effect on the ammeter, we use: A3 = A1 + A2

Why is A1= 0?

We know A1 = 0, so:
A3 = 0 + 0.3 = 0.3 A.   So ammeter A3 reads only 0.3 A.

Your turn

2

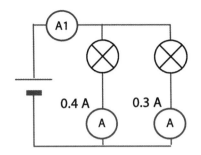

What is the reading on ammeter A1?

Explain your answer.

3

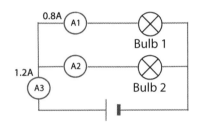

i) What is the reading on ammeter A2?

ii) How would the reading on ammeter A2 change if another bulb was added between A2 and bulb 2?

4

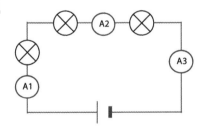

How do the readings on the ammeters compare?

The bulbs are identical.

A A1 = A2 = A3

B A1 > A2 > A3

C A1 = A3, and bigger than A2

2.3 Bulb Brightness

1 In the circuit 1, the ammeter A1 reads 0.3A.
In circuit 2 a second bulb is added.

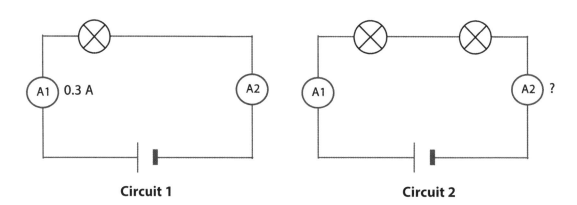

Circuit 1   **Circuit 2**

What do the ammeters in circuit 2 read?

A > 0.3 A   **B** 0.3 A   **C** < 0.3 A

 Detect

I need to understand how an extra bulb changes the current.

What is the
current in A2
in the first
circuit?

 Recall

1. Current is a flow of electrons. The flow and the current are the same everywhere in a loop.
2. Each bulb has resistance and reduces the current.
3. The wire in a bulb gets hot and lights up. So the bulb transfers energy from the circuit as heat and light.

Why
doesn't it
matter where
the ammeter
and bulbs
are?

 Solve

As current is the same all around a series circuit, each ammeter reads the same. Adding a bulb increases the resistance. Increasing the resistance reduces the current.

So the current with two bulbs will be less than 0.3A.

The answer is **C** - less than 0.3 A.

Your turn

2

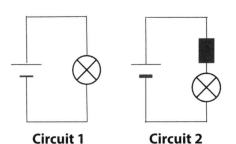

Circuit 1   **Circuit 2**

In which circuit is the bulb brighter?

A   Circuit 1
B   Circuit 2
C   The brightness is the same

3

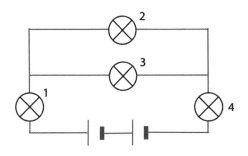

How do the bulbs in this circuit compare in brightness?
(They are all the same kind).

A   Bulb 1 is brightest
B   Bulbs 2 and 3 are brightest
C   Bulbs 1 and 4 are brightest
D   All bulbs are equally bright

4

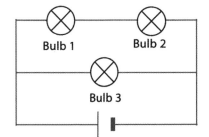

How does the brightness of bulbs 1,2 and 3 compare?

A   All bulbs are equally bright
B   Bulb 1 and 2 are brightest
C   Bulb 3 is brightest

2.4 Batteries to Bulbs

1 Paul set up these circuits. Rank them in order, from brightest to dimmest bulbs.

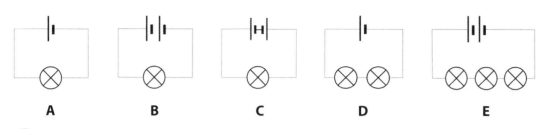

 Detect

I need to decide how the number of bulbs and batteries affects the current.

Why is this true?

 Recall

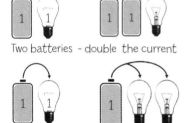
Two batteries - double the current

Two bulbs - half the current

Three bulbs - 1/3 of the current

No current

1. Batteries and current: a battery makes current move around the circuit. The more batteries, the bigger the current.

2. Bulbs and current: each bulb adds resistance to the current flowing. The more bulbs there are, the more resistance there is, and the smaller the current.

3. When two batteries are in opposite directions they cannot make current flow. They cancel out.

Why is it this order?

Solve

Let's compare the currents :
Current in B = Double the current in A
Current in D = Half the current in A
Current in C = O

Current in E: 2 batteries make 2x the current. 3 bulbs make 1/3 of the current. With 2 batteries and 3 bulbs, the effects combine: 2x and 1/3. That makes 2/3. So the current in E is 2/3 of the current in A. And current in E > current in D

The order from brightest to dimmest is: B, A, E, D, C.

Your turn

2 Paul set up these circuits with resistors and ammeters. Rank them in order of the ammeter reading, from largest to smallest.

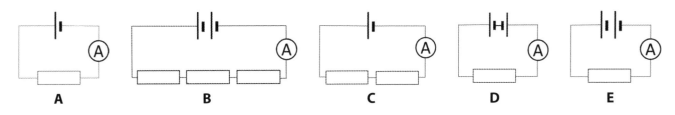

3

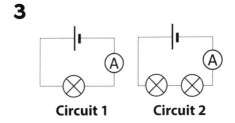

John set up circuits 1 and 2 and recorded the ammeter readings. Draw a diagram of another circuit where the current is:

i) More than in circuit 1

ii) The same as in circuit 2

iii) Less than in circuit 1, but more than in circuit 2.

You can use different combinations of batteries and bulbs.

4

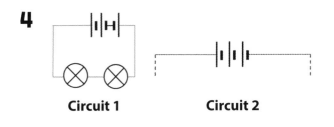

In circuit 1, a battery has been connected the wrong way round. Complete circuit 2 by choosing the number and arrangement of bulbs so they all have the same brightness as in circuit 1.

2.5 Mixed up problems

1 Neil wants to put a switch in this circuit to turn on all the lights at once. Draw a circuit diagram to shows how he can do this.

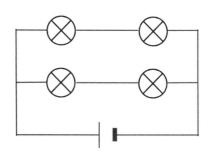

2 Kyle closes different combinations of switches in this circuit. The table shows the current in the ammeter.

What do you think the ammeter will read if he closes switches D, E and F?

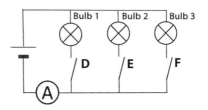

Switches closed	Ammeter reading (A)
D	0.8
D and E	1.4
D and F	1.7

3 The two bulbs in this circuit are made by different companies. Bulb P is bright and Q is dim.

Explain what will happen to the brightness if the bulb positions are swapped.

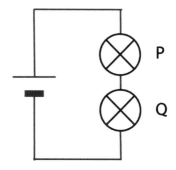

| 1 | /3 | 2 | /3 | 3 | /3 | no hints: +1 | Total | /10 |

4

Bulb1

 i) In which circuit do the bulb(s) have the same brightness as bulb 1?

ii) In which circuit are the bulb(s) brightest?

iii) In which circuit are the bulbs dimmer than bulb 1?

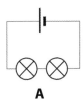

A

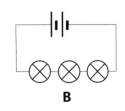

B

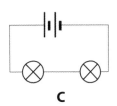

C

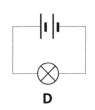

D

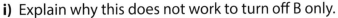

5 Rich wants a switch in this circuit that turns off only bulb B. He puts the switch in position Z.

i) Explain why this does not work to turn off B only.

ii) Redraw the circuit with the switch in a position that works.

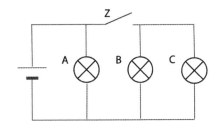

6 Sai draws this diagram but does not make clear which ammeter reads 0.4 A.

Is it ammeter A1 or A2? Explain your choice.

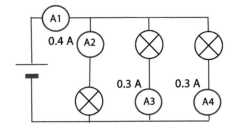

| 1 | /3 | 2 | /3 | 3 | /3 | no hints: +1 Total | /10 |

3.1 Identify energy change

1 A car sits at the top of a hill. The driver releases the brakes and the car rolls down.

As it picks up speed, it also heats up.

Which diagram shows the energy stores of the car

i) At the top **ii)** At the bottom?

GPE = Gravitational potential

KE = Kinetic

TH = Thermal

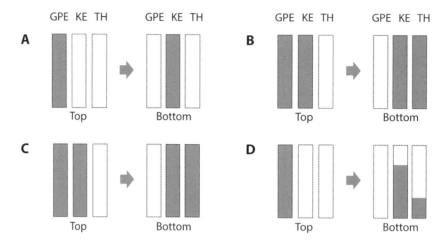

 Detect

I need to work out the energy stores before and after the change.

 Recall

Which stores are filled at the beginning?

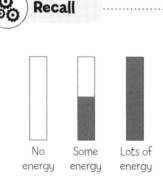

No energy   Some energy   Lots of energy

1. The height of the shaded bars compares how much energy is in each store.
2. Energy is never destroyed. During a change it is transferred from one store to another.
3. Raising an object fills its GPE store (car at the top).
4. Fuel has energy in the chemical store (petrol)
5. An object that starts moving fills its KE store (car rolling down)
6. An object that heats up fills its thermal store.

Solve

What else is wrong about B?

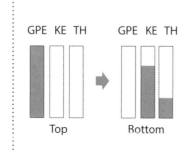

GPE KE TH   GPE KE TH

Top   Bottom

The car is not moving at the top, so it has no KE stored. As the car moves it heats up and so fills its thermal store.

B and C are wrong. They show the car having KE at the top.

A is wrong. It shows no energy in the thermal store.

So D must be correct. Some of the GPE moves to KE. The rest moves to the thermal store.

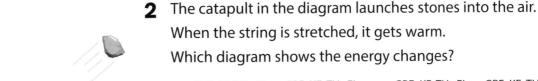

Your turn

2 The catapult in the diagram launches stones into the air.
When the string is stretched, it gets warm.
Which diagram shows the energy changes?

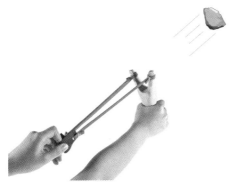

GPE = Gravitational potential

KE = Kinetic

TH = Thermal

EL = Elastic

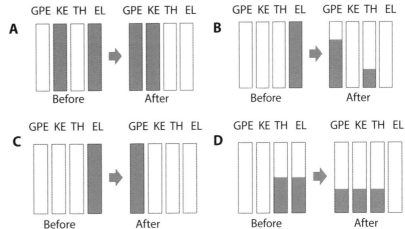

3 The image shows a Sankey diagram. The size of the arrows
represent the amount of energy. A light bulb transfers 100 J
from its electrical store to light (75 J) and heat (25 J).
Draw a Sankey diagram to show this energy change.

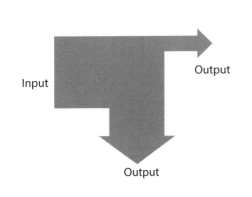

Input

Output

Output

4 Jan cooks dinner in a gas oven. Which answer describes the
energy changes taking place? Explain your choice.

	Stores that decrease	Stores that increase
A	Electrical	Thermal - food and pot
B	Electrical	Thermal - food and air
C	Chemical	Thermal - food and pot
D	Chemical	Thermal - food, pot, air

1	/3	2	/3	3	/3	no hints: +1 Total	/10

Example

3.2 Energy in, energy out

1 Misha eats two chocolate 'Mastery Bars' and goes for a walk. The tables show the contents of the bar and the energy for different activities.

MASTERY BAR

NUTRITION INFORMATION
Serving Size 1 Bar (70g)

Typical values	Per 100 g	Per 70 g
Energy	1446 kJ 346 kcal	1012 kJ 242 kcal
Fat	7.6 g	5.3 g
Carbohydrate	38 g	27 g
Fibre	7.7 g	5.4 g
Protein	33 g	23 g
Salt	0.12 g	0.08 g

Activity	Energy per minute (kJ)
Sitting	6
Standing	7
Eating	6
Walking	15
Running	30

How long does it take Misha to transfer all the energy in the bars by walking?

 Detect

I need to calculate how many minutes of activity transfers the energy in the bars.

 Recall

Which value in the formula is unknown?

1. 1. All the energy from the bars is transferred to activity: Energy in = Energy out

2. Energy in is the energy in two Mastery Bars. Each has 1012 kJ. so two bars have 2024 kJ.

3. Energy out is the energy that walking uses. I can calculate this with a formula:

Energy out = energy/minute × time (minutes)
= 15 kJ/min x time (minutes)

 Solve

How did I work this out?

2024 kJ   2024 kJ

Energy in = energy out.
Energy in = 2 x 1012 = 2024 kJ.
From the formula, energy out must also be 2024 kJ.

The formula for energy out is:
Energy out = 15 kJ/minute × time (minutes)

So if energy in = energy out
2024 kJ = 15 kJ × time (minutes)

Make time the subject of the formula:
time (minutes) = 2024 ÷ 15 = 134.93 minutes
Or 135 minutes.

Your turn

2 How long does it take to transfer the energy in two 70g `Mastery Bars' by running? Use the information from question 1.

MASTERY BAR

MASTERY BAR

Use the tables below for question 3 and question 4.

	Nutritional information		
	Per serving - 50 g	**Per serving - with skim milk**	**Per 100 g**
Energy	700 kJ	900 kJ	1400 kJ

Activity	Energy per minute (kJ)
Sitting	6
Standing	7
Eating	6
Walking	15
Running	30

3 **i)** Ben eats two servings of cereal with skimmed milk. How much energy is stored in the food?
ii) How long does it take Ben to convert the energy from the cereal if he just sits?

4 Ben eats two servings of cereal with skimmed milk. He runs for 30 minutes. Then he walks to school for 40 minutes. How much energy from the cereal is left over?

3.3 Gravitational & Kinetic

1 The diagram shows a car at different places on a roller coaster track. At position A, the car is at rest and its energy is 100 kJ.

i) What is the car's gravitational potential energy at A, B and C?

ii) What is the car's kinetic energy at A, B and C?

Assume no energy is wasted as heat.

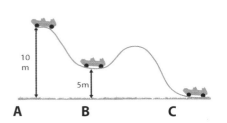

10 m

5m

A   B   C

🔍 Detect

I need to think how energy changes between the gravitational potential energy (GPE) and kinetic energy (KE) stores.

⚙️ Recall

How much energy is GPE and how much KE?

Energy moves from GPE to KE

10m

5m

Total = 100 KJ

Total energy	
GPE	KE

1. The car has GPE and KE. Energy moves from one store to the other during its journey.

2. KE depends on speed. KE = 0 at rest. As the object speeds up, KE increases.

3. GPE depends on height. When the object loses height, GPE decreases. GPE = 0 on the ground

4. No energy is lost. So the total amount of energy in the two stores is the same as at the start.

💡 Solve

How does the difference in height help solve this?

A

100 kJ	
?	0J
GPE	KE

ii) KE = 0 J because the car is not moving.

i) So all the 100 KJ must be GPE.

B

100 kJ	
?	?
GPE	KE

i) The height is reduced by half which means GPE is half the original.
GPE = 1/2×100 =50 kJ

ii) The remaining 50 kJ must be KE.

C

100 kJ	
0 kJ	?
GPE	KE

i) GPE = 0 J as the car is at the bottom.

ii) So all the 100 kJ must be KE.

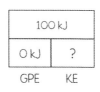

Your turn

2

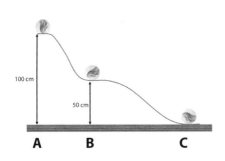

Joel releases a marble from rest at the top of the slope.

It starts at A with 0.5 J of energy.

How much kinetic energy will it have at **i)** B and **ii)** C?

Assume no energy is wasted as heat.

3 The drawings below show a weightlifter dropping a heavy weight.

At which point does the weight:

i) Have the most kinetic energy?

ii) Have the most gravitational potential energy?

iii) Have equal amounts of both?

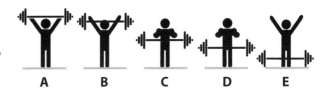

4

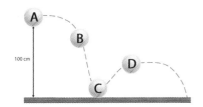

A tennis ball bounces on the ground. At which point is its:

i) Gravitational potential energy highest?

ii) Kinetic energy highest?

iii) Gravitational potential energy increasing?

iv) Kinetic energy increasing?

3.4 Temperature change

1 Sam mixes buckets of hot and cold water. He quickly measures the temperature.

i) Buckets with the same mass of water

1 kg water at 80 °C 1 kg water at 20 °C

ii) Buckets with different masses of water

2 kg water at 80 °C  1 kg water at 20 °C

What will the final temperature after mixing be for **i)**, and for **ii)** ?

A	B	C	D	E
20 °C	40 °C	50 °C	60 °C	80 °C

 Detect

I need to know how to combine temperatures when hot and cold liquids mix.

 Recall

1. Temperature tells you the average energy of the particles.

Why is this true?

The hotter the water, the greater the energy of particles

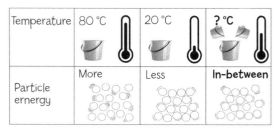

Temperature	80 °C	20 °C	? °C
Particle ernergy	More	Less	**In-between**

When mixed,
- hot water cools
- cold water warms
- particle energy is in-between

 Solve

i) When equal amounts of are mixed, the average energy of the particles is half way between that of the hot and cold water. So the final temperature will also be mid way between the hot water (80 °C) and cold water (20 °C). So it is 50 °C.

ii) When there is twice as much hot water, the average energy of the particles is closer to that of the hot water. So the final temperature will be closer to the hot water than to the cold. The answer is D, because 60 °C is closer to 80 °C.

How did I work out it's 60 °C?

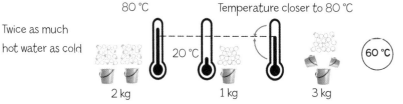

2 Two buckets of water are mixed. Which answer gives the best estimate of the final temperature?

A	B	C	D	E
20 °C	40 °C	50 °C	60 °C	80 °C

90 °C   10 °C

3 Two cups of water are mixed. Which answer gives the best estimate of the final temperature?

A	B	C	D	E
20 °C	40 °C	50 °C	60 °C	80 °C

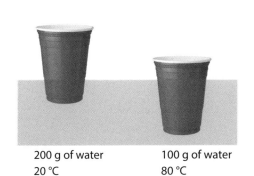

200 g of water   100 g of water
20 °C   80 °C

4 Nadia has 200 g of hot tea at 80 °C. She cools it down by adding cold water at 20 °C.
She immediately measures the temperature and finds it is 60 °C.
How much cold water did she add?

A	B	C	D
100 g	200 g	300 g	400 g

3.5 Temperature Graphs

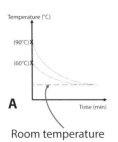

1 Two beakers of hot water are left to cool.

Which set of graphs shows how the temperatures change with time?

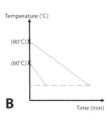 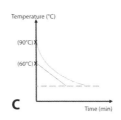 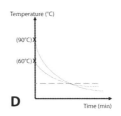 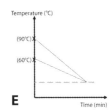

A Room temperature   **B**   **C**   **D**   **E**

 Detect

I need to work out how quickly the temperature drops, and when cooling stops.

 **Recall**

Why does the beaker cool?

Energy moves from the hot object to the cooler room

1. When there is a temperature difference between two objects, energy moves from the hotter to the cooler one.
2. The bigger the difference in temperature, the faster energy moves.
3. The change stops when there is no difference in temperature.

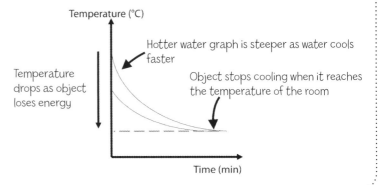

Temperature drops as object loses energy

Hotter water graph is steeper as water cools faster

Object stops cooling when it reaches the temperature of the room

---

 Solve

Why doesn't 60 °C water cool faster?

B & E are wrong because they show the temperatures dropping as a straight line.

C is wrong because it doesn't show the hotter 90 °C water cooling faster.

D is wrong because it shows the hotter water cooling below room temperature.

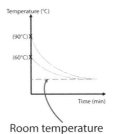

Room temperature

A is correct
- It shows the 90 °C water cooling down faster
- It shows both beakers stop cooling at room temperature.

Your turn

2 Two beakers of cold water are left in a room. One has a temperature of 5 °C and the other 15 °C.

Which graph best how the beakers warm up? Explain your choice.

100ml   100ml

5 °C.   15 °C.

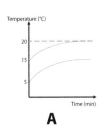

A

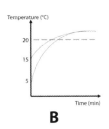

B

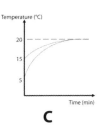

C

3 Tom wants to know whether coffee cools quicker if you add the cold milk immediately, or add it later.

The solid line on the graph shows how the temperature changed when he added milk immediately.

Sketch how you think the graph of temperature would look if Tom added the milk after 5 minutes.

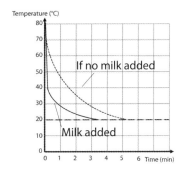

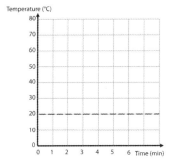

4 Two beakers of hot water at 90 °C are left to cool. Beaker A is insulated, beaker B is not. The graph shows how the temperature of beaker A changes. Sketch on the same axes how the temperature of beaker B would change. The beakers contain equal volumes of water.

Beaker A   Beaker B

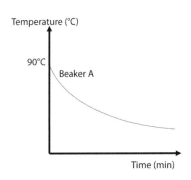

| 1 | /3 | 2 | /3 | 3 | /3 | no hints: +1 Total | /10 |

3.6 Interpret energy diagrams

1 The petrol that powers a car comes from crude oil. The diagram shows what happens for every 100 Joules of energy that is stored in crude oil.

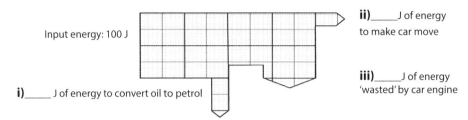

Input energy: 100 J

ii)_____J of energy to make car move

iii)_____J of energy 'wasted' by car engine

i)_____ J of energy to convert oil to petrol

Complete the diagram by adding the correct energy values for **i)**, **ii)** and **iii)**.

🔎 Detect

I need to work out how much energy each square represents.

⚙️ Recall

Is any of the input energy lost?

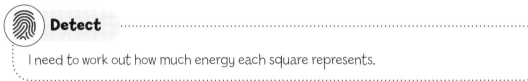

Source

Loses chemical energy

Energy flowchart   Energy stores

Input energy – chemical   Useful energy – kinetic energy

Wasted energy - heat and sound

20 little squares   If 20 little squares of energy represent 100 J, each one represents 5 J

1. There are different ways to show energy.

2. In a Sankey diagram, the arrows show where the input energy is transferred.

3. The width of the arrows represent the amount of energy.

💡 Solve

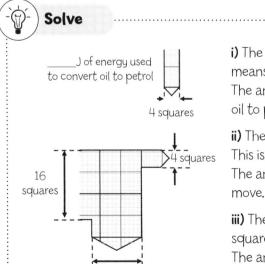

_____J of energy used to convert oil to petrol

4 squares

16 squares

4 squares

12 squares

i) The width of the arrow is 4 squares. Each square means 5 J. So 4 squares means 4 x 5 = 20 J.
The answer is: 20 J of energy are used to convert oil to petrol.

ii) The energy to make the car move is 4 squares. This is 4 x 5 J = 20 J.
The answer is: 20 J of energy to make the car move.

iii) The energy wasted by the car engine is 12 squares. This is 12 x 5 J = 60 J.
The answer is: 60 J of energy wasted by the car engine.

Your turn

2 The Sankey diagram shows an energy transfer for an electrical device to lift heavy objects.

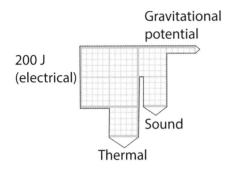

Gravitational potential

200 J (electrical)

Sound

Thermal

i) How much of the 200 J does it transfer to the thermal store?

ii) How much of the 200 J does it transfer to the gravitational potential store?

3 A car is travelling at 30mph. It then drives up a hill, puts on its brakes, and stops at the top. Which energy stores diagram shows the energy before and after the car climbs the hill?

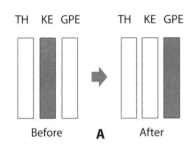

Before **A** After

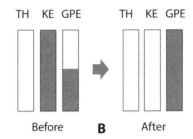

Before **B** After

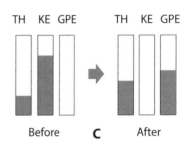

Before **C** After

TH = Thermal

KE = Kinetic

GPE = Gravitational Potential

4 The flowchart shows energy moving through a mystery device. Which of these is it likely to be?

A A loudspeaker playing music

B An electronic doorbell

C A tablet playing a movie

D A solar-powered calculator

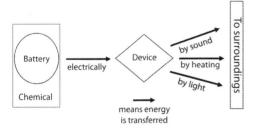

Battery

Chemical

electrically

Device

by sound

by heating

by light

To surroundings

→ means energy is transferred

3.7 Identify wasted energy

1 Jude has a battery-powered robot dog. It walks and barks. When she picks it up, it feels warm.

Draw an energy diagram for the robot dog.

Show **i)** the input and output stores

ii) the useful and wasted energy.

 Detect

I need to work out where the energy is stored before and after the change.

 Recall

Which are input and which output energies?

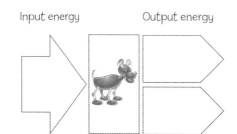

Input energy   Output energy

1. The toy dog's energy comes from the battery.

2. The dog has energy because it moves, it barks, and it gets hot.

3. Energy is transferred from one store to another, but not lost. So,

Input energy = output energy

 Solve

Why are the output arrows different sizes?

Input energy comes from the battery. This energy is in the chemical store.

Output energy:
• dog moving = kinetic energy
• dog barks = sound
• dog gets hot = thermal or heat

The toy is designed to move and bark. So kinetic energy and sound are useful
The toy is not designed to get hot. Heat is wasted energy.

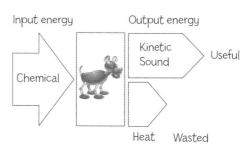

Input energy   Output energy

Chemical   Kinetic Sound   Useful

Heat   Wasted

2 Ben listens to a cartoon story on his tablet. The tablet feels hot afterwards.

Draw an energy diagram to show:
i) the input and output energy stores.
ii) the useful and wasted energy stores.

3 A motor is used to lift up a load.
i) Describe how energy could be wasted in this device.
ii) Draw a diagram to show the energy transfers taking place.

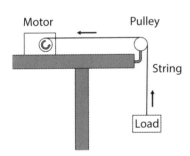

4 The diagram shows a new rollercoaster. The biggest hill is at the beginning and the top of each loop is a little lower than the one before.
Explain why the loops have to get lower using the idea of wasted energy.

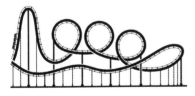

| 1 | /3 | 2 | /3 | 3 | /3 | no hints: +1 Total | /10 |

3.8 Calculate efficiency

1 The table shows energy data for two car engines.

Engine	Input energy: chemical store (kJ)	Output energy: heat (kJ)	Output energy: kinetic store (kJ)
A	150	120	30
B	60	40	20

i) Which engine is more efficient? Explain your answer.

ii) 200 kJ of energy is supplied to both engines. How much kinetic energy do they transfer?

 Detect

I need to identify the useful energy and use the efficiency formula.

Recall

Which energy is useful?

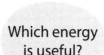

1. Efficiency means how much of the input energy an object transfers to useful output energy, or

Efficiency = $\dfrac{\text{Useful output energy}}{\text{Input energy}}$

2. Efficiency is a number less than 1. Useful energy is less than input energy because some energy is always wasted.

Solve

Why is Engine B more efficient?

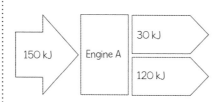

i) The useful energy is movement or kinetic energy (30 kJ). The wasted energy is heat (120 kJ)

Engine A Efficiency = 30 kJ/150 kJ = 1/5. 0.2 or 20% of the input is transferred usefully.

Engine B Efficiency = 20 kJ/60 kJ = 1/3 0.33 or 33% of the input is transferred usefully.

The answer is: engine B is more efficient.

ii) Engine A transfers 0.2 of the energy to kinetic. For 200 kJ, kinetic energy is 0.2 x 200 = 40 kJ.

Engine B transfers 0.33 of the energy to kinetic. For 200 kJ, kinetic energy is 0.33 x 200 = 66 kJ.

Your turn

2 The table shows energy data for two car engines.

Engine	Chemical energy from fuel (kJ)	Thermal energy (kJ)	Kinetic energy (kJ)
A	200	150	50
B	200	80	120

i) Which engine is less efficient? Explain your answer.

ii) 400 kJ of chemical energy is supplied to the engines. How much kinetic energy does each one produce?

3 Ravi pushes a car up a hill. He transfers 600kJ of energy from his chemical store.
The car gains 150kJ as kinetic energy. 450KJ is wasted as heat.
Calculate the efficiency of the energy transfer.

4 A young cow eats a tuft of grass that contains 200 kJ of energy.
20 kJ of the energy is used for growth. The rest is lost to the environment.
Calculate the efficiency of the energy transfer.

3.9 Mixed up problems

1 The flowchart shows a series of energy changes.

Which situation could the flowchart be describing?

A A fire for keeping people warm

B A cooker for heating water

C A fire for heating water

D A stove for warming a room.

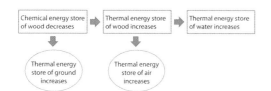

2 The table shows how much energy a cereal provides and the energy used for different activities.

i) How much Popsicles cereal does Max need to eat to provide the energy for 100 minutes of standing?

ii) Max eats one serving with skim milk. How long can he run for on that energy?

POPSICLES breakfast cereal
Nutrition Information

	1 serving with milk	100g of cereal
Energy	900 kJ	1400 kJ

Activity	Energy per minute (kJ)
Sitting	6
Standing	7
Walking	15
Running	30

3 Zoe on the swing has 500 J of energy. As she moves from A to B she transfers 400 J from her gravitational potential store.

At B, how much energy is in her:

i) Gravitational potential store

ii) Kinetic energy store?

Assume no energy is wasted as heat.

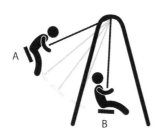

| 1 | /3 | 2 | /3 | 3 | /3 | no hints: +1 Total | /10 |

Practice

0 °C   20 °C

4 Joel quickly adds 100g of ice to 200g of cold drink. What is the best estimate of the new temperature?

A	B	C	D	E
0 °C	5 °C	10 °C	15 °C	20 °C

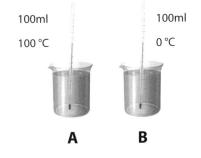

100ml   100ml

100 °C   0 °C

A   **B**

5 Two beakers are left in a room at 20 °C. Beaker A has water at 100 °C. The graph shows how its temperature changes. Beaker B contains the same volume of water at 0 °C. Sketch how its temperature changes on the same axes.

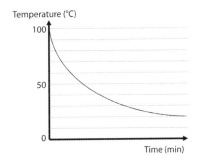

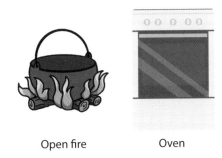

Open fire   Oven

6 Bo cooks a baked potato on an open fire. She notices it takes longer to cook than in her oven at home.
i) Draw an energy diagram for the open fire. Label the input and output energy, and useful and wasted energy.
ii) How would an energy diagram for the cooker be different?
iii) Explain why it takes longer to cook on an open fire.

4.1 Gravity and distance

1

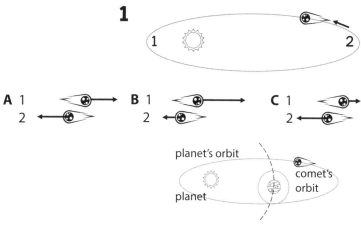

As a comet orbits the Sun, it experiences a gravitational force.

i) Which diagram shows the size of the force from the sun at points 1 and 2?

A 1
2

B 1
2

C 1
2

planet's orbit

comet's orbit

planet

ii) The comet passes close to a planet. It starts to orbit the planet instead of the Sun. Explain how this could happen, using the idea of gravity.

Detect

I need to think how gravitational forces change with distance.

Recall

 Which gravitational force is the biggest?

Closer to Sun = stronger gravity

Further from Sun = weaker gravity

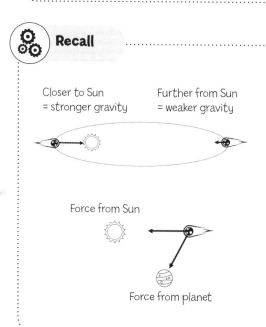

Force from Sun

Force from planet

1. There is a strong gravitational force on an object (comet) near a very large mass (Sun). This force keeps the comet in orbit.
2. The size of gravitational force depends on how far the two objects are apart. The closer they are, the stronger the force.
3. The size of the force changes with mass. The greater the mass of the objects, the stronger the gravitational force.
4. An object (comet) can feel two gravitational forces (from the Sun and from a planet). Which one is bigger depends on their distance and mass.

Solve

1
2

i) At position 1, the comet is closest to the Sun. So the gravitational force is strongest.
At position 2, the comet is furthest from the Sun. So the gravitational force is weakest.
So the answer is B.

Why does the force from the planet get bigger?

ii) The comet orbits the Sun because the Sun's gravitational force is the strongest. When the comet goes very close to the planet, its gravitational force gets very big – bigger than the Sun's.
This makes the comet orbit the planet instead of the Sun.

2 A satellite orbits the Earth.

At which position is the gravitational force largest?

Put positions 1, 2 and 3 in order, from largest to smallest force.

3 **i)** A comet travels close to Uranus, and gets trapped in orbit around the planet. Complete the diagram to show what happens to its path.

ii) Jupiter and Saturn are the two planets in our solar system most likely to trap a comet. Explain why.

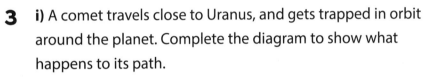

4 A rock lies between Earth and the Moon. At position 1, the gravitational forces from Earth and the Moon are equal.

Which diagram shows the size of the forces on it at position 2? Explain your choice.

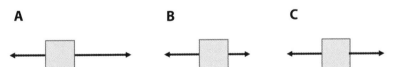

A   B   C

| 1 | /3 | 2 | /3 | 3 | /3 | no hints: +1 Total | /10 |

4.2 Daylight & seasons

1 These maps show which parts of the world have daylight at three times during one day. The location marker and times are for London.

i) What season is it in London?

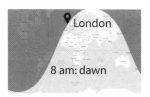
8 am: dawn

12 pm: noon

3pm: dusk

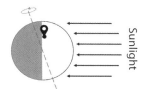

ii) This globe shows sunlight hitting London on the same day as i).

Explain how the season affects its daylight hours and temperature. Add labels and text to the globe.

 Detect

I need to think how the Earth's rotation affects daylight hours and temperature.

 Recall

What is the season in the southern hemisphere?

Daylight
8 am - 3pm

1. The band of daylight moves towards the East.
2. The left map shows daylight starting in London, and the right map daylight ending. Day time (7 hours) is much shorter than night time (17 hours).
3. Day time is far longer in the southern hemisphere, as shown by the wide band of light.
4. The northern hemisphere tilts away from the Sun.
5. The Sun's energy is more spread out in the northern hemisphere than in the southern hemisphere. This makes the temperature lower in the hemisphere tilted away from the Sun.
6. As London rotates about the dotted axis, it has a short day and a longer night.

 Solve

i) Less than half of the line level with London is in daylight. Day length is only 7 hours on London's rotation around the Earth's axis. 17 hours are in darkness. This means the season is winter.

ii)

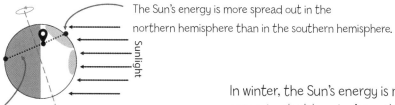

The Sun's energy is more spread out in the northern hemisphere than in the southern hemisphere.

What shows how the Sun's energy is spread out?

The dashed lines show London's path. Most of the time it is on the shaded side (night). So day time is shorter than night time.

In winter, the Sun's energy is more spread out at London's position. So it receives less energy and the temperature is colder.

Your turn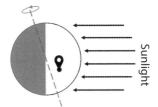

2

A student goes on holiday to Australia in December.
Add labels and lines to the globe to explain how the season affects the day length and temperature in Australia.

3 The equinox is a day when there are equal numbers of day time and night time hours across the world.
Which picture shows midday in London during an equinox? Explain your answer.

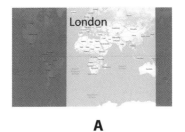

A

B

C

4

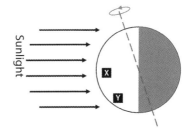

The ouput energy of a solar panel is 50 J per second at position X.
How would the output energy change if the solar panel was moved to position Y? Explain your answer.

4.3 Changing appearance

1 Noah views the Moon from Earth through a telescope. Diagrams **i)**, **ii)** and **iii** show the positions of the Moon on different days of the month.

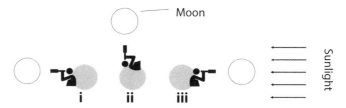

For **i)**, **ii)** and **iii**, choose the diagram below that shows how Noah sees the Moon.

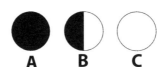

A   B   C

 Detect

I need to imagine myself in each position to know how the Moon appears.

 Recall

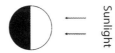

Which part looks bright?

(It looks like Earth is blocking the Moon, but that's because the diagram is not drawn to scale and 2D)

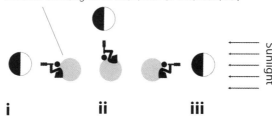

i   ii   iii

1. We know that the sunlight comes from the right.

2. The right side of the moon is always bright and the left side always dark.

3. We know that Noah can only see the side facing him. So I can colour in each Moon to show its bright and dark side.

 Solve

I imagine myself in each position:

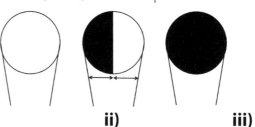

i)

ii)

iii)

Why is it all light in i?

i) I see all the bright side of the Moon. The answer is **C**.

ii) I see half the side that is dark and half the side that is bright. The answer is **B**.

iii) All the sunlight is blocked by Earth. I see only dark. The answer is **A**.

2 A wolf howls at the Moon on four different nights. The diagrams show the positions of the Moon.

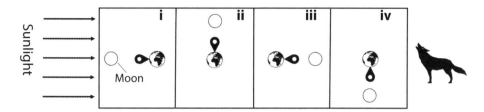

For each position **i)-iv)**, choose the diagram that shows how the Moon looks to the wolf.

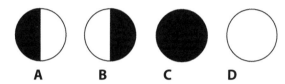

A   **B**   **C**   **D**

3 The diagram shows Venus in different positions as it orbits the Sun.

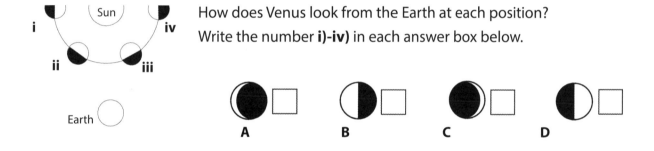

How does Venus look from the Earth at each position?
Write the number **i)-iv)** in each answer box below.

A   **B**   **C**   **D**

4 A space probe took a photograph of Io, a moon of Jupiter. Which diagram shows the correct positions of Io and the space probe? Explain your choice.

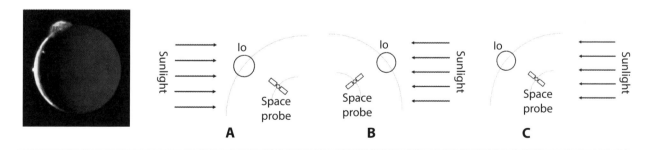

A   **B**   **C**

| 1 | /3 | 2 | /3 | 3 | /3 | no hints: +1 Total | /10 |

 **Example**

4.4 Planetary Orbits

1 The table shows information about Earth and Mars.

Planet	Distance to the Sun (compared to Earth)	Radius of planet (km)	Tilt of Axis (°)
Earth	1.00	6378	23.5
Mars	1.64	3396	25.0

Compare the planets in terms of :

i) Year length

ii) Surface temperature (ignore the effect of the atmosphere)

iii) Changes during the year.

 Detect

I need to decide which data in the table is relevant and how it affects i, ii and iii.

 Recall

Why does tilt change day length?

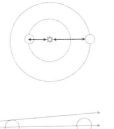

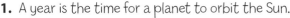

1. A year is the time for a planet to orbit the Sun.
2. Year length depends on the distance of a planet from its star. The greater the distance, the longer the year length.
3. Surface temperature is also related to distance to the star.
4. At a greater distance, less of the sun's radiation reaches the planet.

 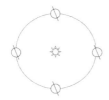

5. Tilt means the planet spins with its poles not pointing up and down. This means that day length changes during the orbit and the planet has seasons.

 Solve

What data is similar for Earth and Mars?

i) Year length. The greater the distance of a planet from its star (Sun), the longer its orbit and the length of a year. Mars is 1.5 times further from the Sun than Earth, so Mars has longer years than Earth.

ii) Surface temperature. As Mars is further from the Sun, less radiation reaches its surface. So it has a lower surface temperature than Earth.

iii) Changes during the year. Both planets spin with their poles tilted. One hemisphere is tilted towards the Sun and has brighter, longer days. The other is tilted away from the Sun and has colder, shorter days.

2 Upsilon Andromeda A is a star that has planets. The table shows the estimated data
for two of its planets, named c and d.

Planet	Distance to Star (compared to Earth -Sun)	Mass (compared to Jupiter)	Tilt (°)
c	241	14	0
d	1276	10	0

Compare the planets c and d in terms of

   i)   Year length

   ii)   Temperature

   iii)   Changes during the year.

3 Eris and Pluto are icy dwarf planets. Their orbits overlap at the edge of the solar system.
Use the diagram to help you fill the table with the numbers below in the correct boxes.

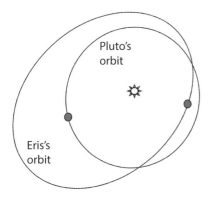

560   **-240**   **-218**   **248**

Dwarf planet	Year length (Earth years)	Surface temperature (°C)
Pluto		
Eris		

4 Dawn was a space probe that visited the asteroid
belt. Juno was a probe sent to Jupiter. Each had
solar panels so they could use the Sun's radiation.
The table shows the energy from the solar panels.

Sketch a diagram to explain the difference in energy
output for the solar panels of Dawn and Juno.

Probe	Distance to sun (Earth years)	Energy output of solar panels (Joules/second)
Dawn	3	1300
Juno	5	500

4.5 Calculate weight

1 A Mars robot travels along a thin metal ramp. It can break if the force on it exceeds 150 N.

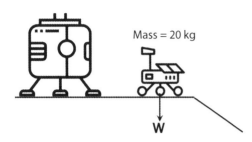

Mass = 20 kg

W

The robot's mass is 20 kg. On Mars its weight, shown by W, is 72 N.
Could the robot use the ramp on Earth without breaking the ramp?
g on Earth = 10 N/kg.

 Detect

I need to calculate the robot's weight on Earth.

 Recall

Why is the robot's weight different on Earth?

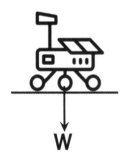

W

1. The force of gravity (weight) pulls downwards on the robot.
2. The robot pushes downwards on the ramp with the same force as its weight.
3. The maximum force the ramp can take is 150 N.
4. The formula for calculating the weight of the robot is:

W = m x g

W is weight, m is mass and g is gravitational field strength.

 Solve

We need to find out whether the robot's weight on Earth is greater than 150 N. The values to put into the weight formula are:

m = 20 kg   (mass is the same everywhere)
g = 10 N/kg (Earth)

Why is the weight of 72 N not used?

So W = m x g becomes
    W = 20 kg x 10 N/kg = 200 N,

As this force is more than 150 N, the ramp might break. So the robot cannot use the ramp on Earth.

2 The ladder of a spacecraft breaks if the weight on it exceeds 500 N. On Mercury, an astronaut can use it safely. She weighs 360 N and her mass is 100 kg.
Can she use the ladder on Earth? Show your calculation.
g on Earth = 10 N/kg.

3 A table designed for the Moon can support a weight of 4 N. Can it support a 2.5 kg laptop on Mars? Explain your answer.
g on Mars = 4 N/kg.

4 On Earth, a dance mat needs a force of 250 N pressing down on it to work.
Would the weight of a 60 kg person work the mat on Venus?
g on Venus = 9 N/kg.

1	/3	2	/3	3	/3	no hints: +1 Total	/10

4.6 Mixed up problems

1 The diagram shows the path of the Juno probe on its way to Jupiter. There are gravitational forces from the Earth, the Sun and Jupiter.

Which one exerts the biggest gravitational force at positions **i)**, **ii)** and **iii)** ? Explain your answers.

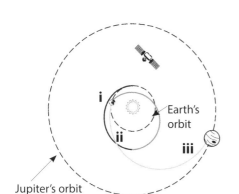

2 Match each daylight map i) and ii) to a season, and globe A or B by drawing lines across.

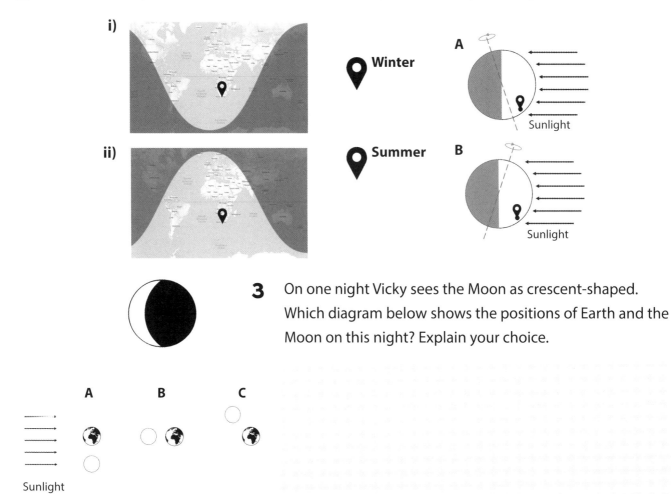

3 On one night Vicky sees the Moon as crescent-shaped. Which diagram below shows the positions of Earth and the Moon on this night? Explain your choice.

| 1 | /3 | 2 | /3 | 3 | /3 | no hints: +1 Total | /10 |

© Mastery Science 2017

4 The tables show patterns in the properties of planets in the solar system. Explain which pattern is caused by the distance of the planets from the Sun.

Planet	Year length (Earth days)	Day length (Earth =1)	Gravity (N/kg)
Mercury	88	59	3.6
Venus	225	243	8.7
Earth	365	1	9.8
Mars	687	1.03	3.7
Jupiter	4332	0.41	25.9
Saturn	10755	0.45	11.3
Uranus	30688	0.72	10.4
Neptune	60190	0.67	14

5 Apollo 17 astronauts collected rock samples from the Moon. The table shows the mass and weight of the rocks that were measured on Earth.

What did the rocks weigh on the Moon?

g on Earth =10/N/kg.

g on Moon = 1.6 N/kg.

Total mass	Total weight
115 kg	1150 N

6 Kepler-186f is a planet that orbits a distant star. The table shows data about the planet.

How does Kepler-186f compare to Earth, in terms of its:

i) Year length   **ii)** Surface temperature (ignore atmospheres)

iii) Changes during the year.

Planet	Distance to Star, the Sun	Tilt of Axis (°)
Earth	1.00	23.5
K-186f	0.39	0

Example

5.1 Chemical change evidence

1 Katie heated different substances to see if there was a chemical change. The table shows her observations.

Name of substance	Observations		
	Before heating (room temperature)	**During heating**	**After cooling**
i) Sodium hydrogen carbonate	White solid	Colourless gas and droplets of colourless liquid form	White solid
ii) Iron nitrate	Pale purple solid	Turns red-brown, brown gas forms	Brown-red solid
iii) Hydrogen peroxide	Colourless liquid	Bubbles form	Colourless liquid

For substances **i)**, **ii)** and **iii)**, explain whether there was a chemical change.

Detect

I need to think what the evidence is for a chemical change.

Why is this evidence?

Recall

In a chemical change, a new substance always forms.

The evidence for a new substance can be:

- ◯ Permanent colour change
- ◯ Fizzing or sign of a new gas
- ◯ Heat or light produced
- ◯ A precipitate (solid) forms if I mix two solutions.

Solve

i) Heating sodium hydrogen carbonate

- ◯ Permanent colour change
- ✓ Fizzing or sign of a new gas
- ◯ Heat or light produced

→ **Chemical change**
The droplets are likely to be water. A colourless gas and water droplets are both evidence for new substances.

ii) Heating iron nitrate

- ✓ Permanent colour change
- ✓ Fizzing or sign of a new gas
- ◯ Heat or light produced

→ **Chemical change**
A permanent colour change and brown gas are both evidence for new substances.

iii) Heating hydrogen peroxide solution

- ◯ Permanent colour change
- ? Fizzing or sign of a new gas
- ◯ Heat or light produced

→ **Not sure**
The bubbles could be a new gas, or due to boiling. There is no other evidence.

Why is the answer 'not sure'?

Your turn

2 Alys mixed different solutions together. The table shows her observations.

	Solution 1	Solution 2	After mixing
i)	Silver nitrate (colourless)	Sodium chloride (colourless)	White precipitate forms
ii)	Copper sulfate (blue)	Dilute sulfuric acid (colourless)	The solution stays blue
iii)	Sodium hydrogen carbonate (colourless)	Hydrochloric acid (colourless)	Fizzing, leaving a colourless solution

For each experiment **i)**, **ii)** and **iii)**, explain whether there was a chemical change.

3 Jason added different substances to water. The table shows his observations.

Experiment	Substance	Before adding water	After adding to water
i)	Sodium metal	Silvery-grey metal	Fizzes, catches fire, solid disappears leaving a colourless solution
ii)	Sodium iodide	White solid	Solid disappears leaving a colourless solution
iii)	Iodine	Silvery-grey solid	A pale orange solution forms. Some solid remains

For each experiment **i)**, **ii)** and **iii)**, explain whether there was a chemical change.

4 Tomas mixed red and blue food colour in a glass of water. The water went purple.
Tomas concluded there was a chemical change because it went a different colour.
Do you think he was correct? Explain your answer.

| 1 | /3 | 2 | /3 | 3 | /3 | no hints: +1 Total | /10 | 57 |

 **Example**

5.2 Physical change evidence

1 Here are some changes:

i) Milk turning sour

ii) Boiling water in an electric kettle

iii) Lighting a match

iv) Diluting orange juice with water.

Which ones are physical changes? Explain your answer.

 Detect

I need to think whether there is evidence of a physical or chemical change.

 Recall

1. A physical change means no new substances are made.
2. The more evidence we have, the more we can be sure which type of change it is.

Why are these evidence?

Evidence of physical change	Evidence of chemical change
Change of state	New substance forms (could be a different colour)
Making a mixture (which can be separated again)	Fizzing (means a new gas has formed)
Easily reversed	Produces heat or light

Solve

i) Milk turning sour

Physical	Chemical
None	The sour taste suggests a new substance

No evidence of physical change

ii) Boiling water in an electric kettle

Physical	Chemical
It's a change of state - liquid to gas	None
It's easily reversed - steam condenses	

Evidence of physical change

Which answer has most evidence?

iii) Lighting a match

Physical	Chemical
None	New substances form
	Produces heat and light

No evidence of physical change

iv) Diluting orange juice with water

Physical	Chemical
It's making a mixture - orange juice + water	None

Evidence of physical change

2 Here are some changes:

i) Making ice in the freezer

ii) Making a cake from eggs, flour and sugar

iii) Bread dough rising

iv) Dissolving sugar in a cup of tea.

Which one(s) are physical changes? Describe your evidence.

3 Here are some more changes:

i) Frying an egg in a pan

ii) Sand mixing with water at the beach

iii) Making sodium bicarbonate fizz with vinegar

iv) A bathroom mirror fogging up after a shower.

Which one(s) are physical changes. Describe your evidence.

4 Students carried out two heating experiments:

Experiment A Jamie heated green copper carbonate powder. It turned black and the powder bubbled. When it cooled down, the powder stayed black.

Experiment B Sheena heated silvery-grey iodine crystals. She saw a purple gas. When the purple gas cooled down it went back to silvery-grey crystals.

Is experiment A or B is more likely to be a physical change? Explain your choice.

5.3 Mass Change

1 Luke heated some magnesium metal. He measured the mass before and after heating. The table shows his results.

Magnesium metal → ← Crucible

Total mass of crucible & magnesium	
Before heating (g)	**After heating** (g)
47.98	48.01

i) State what happened to the mass of the magnesium.

ii) Explain why.

 Detect

I need to think about how a change in mass is evidence of a chemical reaction.

Do substances always get heavier when they react?

 Recall

1. In a chemical reaction at least one new substance forms.
2. A new substance could have a different mass.
3. If mass increases, it suggests another substance chemically combined with it.

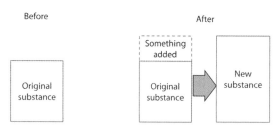

4. If the mass decreases, it suggests that a part of the substance has been lost.

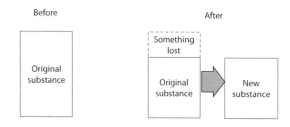

 Solve

Which statement is a conclusion, and which an idea?

i) The mass after heating increased.

The increase = 48.01 - 47.98 = 0.03 g

ii) An increase in mass is evidence of a chemical change.

The increase in mass suggests the magnesium has chemically combined with something. This could be oxygen in the in the air.

Your turn

2

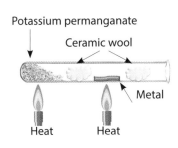

Potassium permanganate
Ceramic wool
Metal
Heat   Heat

The diagram shows how a teacher heated copper metal.

The table shows what happened to the the mass of copper.

Mass of beaker & water	
Before heating (g)	**After heating** (g)
0.050	0.063

Do you think there was a chemical reaction? Explain your answer.

3

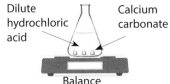

Dilute hydrochloric acid   Calcium carbonate

Balance

Annie put some acid in a flask onto a balance. She added pieces of calcium carbonate and started a timer. The mixture began to fizz. The table shows her results.

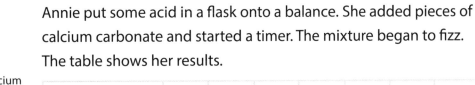

Time (s)	0	30	60	120	180	240	300
Mass of flask & chemicals (g)	90.33	89.97	89.81	89.63	89.53	89.47	89.47

i) What is the evidence for a chemical change?

ii) Describe what you think happened between 240 and 300 seconds.

4

Mass of beaker & water	
Before heating (g)	**After heating** (g)
178	170

Janine heated a beaker of water for 5 minutes. The table shows the mass before and after heating. She concluded that a chemical change took place.

Was Janine right? Explain your answer.

| 1 | /3 | 2 | /3 | 3 | /3 | no hints: +1 Total | /10 |

5.4 Find pH with indicator

1   Some fruits and vegetables can be used as indicators. The chart shows the colours at different pH values.

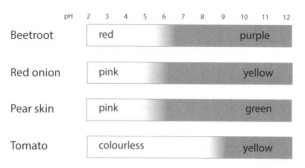

i)   A solution turns green with pear skin indicator. What does this tell you about the pH of the solution?

ii) Which indicator could tell you that the solution is not an acid?

iii) Which indicator could tell you the solution has a pH of 9 or more?

🔎 Detect

I need to work out at what pH the different indicators change colour.

⚙️ Recall

What are the pH ranges of this indicator?

One colour for range pH <4.5   A different colour for range pH > 5.5

Between pH 4.5-5.5, the colour changes

1. Solutions below pH 7 are acidic, and above pH 7 are alkaline.
2. An indicator is a substance used to test the pH of a solution.
3. The indicator has one colour over one pH range, and a different colour over a different pH range.
4. To know if the pH is higher or lower than a certain value, we need an indicator that changes colour around that value.

💡 Solve

Why won't pear skin work for ii) ?

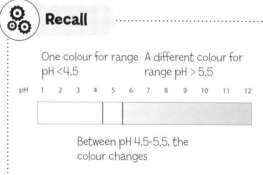

i) Pear skin indicator changes to green at pH 5.5. So if the colour is green, we can tell the pH must be 5.5 or above.

ii) Beetroot indicator changes colour above pH 7. So if a solution goes purple, we know that its pH is 7 or above. This means it is not acidic.

iii) Tomato indicator changes colour around pH 9. So if a solution goes yellow, we know that the pH must be 9 or above.

2 Explain which indicator would be most suitable to detect an acid that is pH 3 or below.

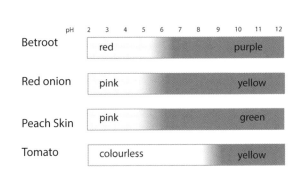

3 A liquid turns red onion indicator dark, and tomato indicator light. What range of pH could the liquid have?

4 **i)** A chemical turned litmus paper red. What does this tell you about its pH?

   i) The diagram shows the ranges of three indicators. Which one could show you that a solution has a pH more than 4? Explain your choice.

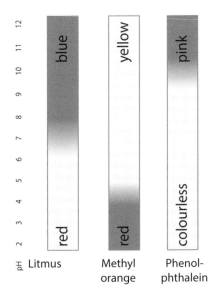

5.5 Make solutions neutral

1 Hydrangea flowers go different colours depending on the pH of the soil. Sean's flowers are deep blue. Emma's are purple-pink.

Colour of flower	Deep blue			Purple-pink			Deep pink
Soil pH	4.5	5	5.5	6	6.5	6.8	7

Sean and Emma both want their hydrangeas to be deep pink.

i) What substance should they add to the soil?

ii) Who needs to add more substance to their soil? Explain your answer.

 Detect

I need to work out how to change the pH of a solution.

 Recall

1. pH 7 is neutral.
2. pH values below 7 are acidic. The lower the pH, the more acidic the solution.
3. pH values above 7 are alkaline. The higher the pH, the more alkaline the solution.

1	2	3	4	5	6	7	8	9	10	11	12	13	14

More acidic   Neutral   More alkaline

 What does pH tell you?

4. Adding alkali raises the pH. It can neutralise an acidic solution.
5. Adding acid lowers the pH. It can neutralise an alkaline solution.

 Solve

How does adding alkali change pH ?

i) Sean's soil is around pH 4.5. Emma's soil is around pH 6. The soils are both acidic. Both Sean and Emma need to raise the pH to make the soil pH 7 - neutral. They can do this by adding an alkali to their soil, which neutralises the acid.

ii) Sean's soil has a lower pH than Emma's. So the pH needs to change more to be neutralised. So Sean needs to add more alkali.

Your turn

2 Siena's soil has pH 9 and Louis' soil has pH 11. Deep pink hydrangeas need a pH of 7 or more.

i) Explain what they both need to add to their soil to get deep pink hydrangeas.

ii) Should they both add the same amount? Explain your answer.

3 Bees, wasps and ants use acidic and alkaline stings to defend themselves.

Bee sting pH 5   Wasp sting pH 10   Ant sting pH 3

The table shows three household substances and their pH.

Name of substance	pH
Vinegar	4
Bicarbonate of soda	9
Water	7

Which of the three substances could you use to neutralise:

i) A bee sting. **ii)** A wasp sting. **iii)** An ant sting. Give a reason for your choices.

4 Neutrax is a product for cleaning up acid spills. It contains an indicator that changes colour as shown in the table.

pH	1	2-4	5-6	7	8-9	10-12	13-14
Colour of indicator	Red	Orange	Yellow	Green	Blue/Green	Blue	Purple

i) Apart from an indicator, what other substance does Neutrax contain to clean up acid spills?

ii) How do you know when Neutrax has cleaned up all the acid?

| 1 | /3 | 2 | /3 | 3 | /3 | no hints: +1 Total | /10 |

5.6 Mixed up problems

1 Two students heated a piece of white, calcium carbonate. It glowed with a bright light. A white solid was left behind.
Jamie: *"There was evidence of a chemical change".*
Adi: *"There was not enough evidence of a chemical change".*
Who do you think was correct? Give a reason.

2 Peter heated water in a flask and saw bubbles form. He decided this was a chemical change because a new gas formed.
Do you think Peter was correct? Explain your answer.

Mass of powder		
Before heating (g)	After 2 minutes (g)	After 4 minutes (g)
5.0	3.2	3.2

3 Ahmed weighed some green copper carbonate. Then he heated it strongly in a test tube for two minutes.
He noticed the powder turn black. He weighed the powder and heated it for a further 2 minutes. It did not change colour again.
i) What is the evidence for a chemical change after 2 minutes?
ii) Was there a chemical change between 2 and 4 minutes? Give a reason.

1 /3 2 /3 3 /3 no hints: +1 Total / 10 © Mastery Science 2017

4 Your stomach contains acid to help digestion and kill bacteria. Too much acid in the stomach can cause painful indigestion.

i) Explain how an indigestion tablet could work to stop indigestion.

ii) Explain why taking too many indigestion tablets could increase the chances of food poisoning.

5 Litmus paper can test if a solution is acidic or alkaline. The table shows the colour changes of red and blue litmus paper. How would you use litmus paper to show that a substance is neutral?

Type of litmus paper	Colour in acid	Colour in neutral solution	Colour in alkali
Red	Red	Red	Blue
Blue	Red	Blue	Blue

6 Chemical changes take place in the leaves of oak trees during the year.

Write down some evidence for this claim.

6.1 Identify dyes

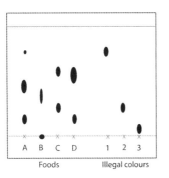

A B C D   1 2 3

Foods   Illegal colours

1 Food analysts use chromatography to check whether food colours are legal. The diagram shows a chromatogram for foods, A, B , C and D.

i) Explain how you can tell that food C contains an illegal colour.

ii) Is there evidence that food A contains an illegal colour? Give a reason.

Detect

I need to interpret the results of a chromatogram.

Recall

How do you two if there are two dyes?

 These dyes are the same as they move the same distance. A single spot means a pure substance.

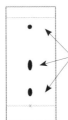 These dyes are different as they move different distances. A mixture contains several substances and each one makes a spot.

 These dyes are the same. The different sized spots mean there are different amounts of dye.

Distance moved by solvent

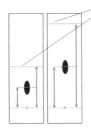 Here, each dye moves half the distance that the solvent moved. This means that the dyes are the same.

Solve

Does it matter if the spot is big or small?

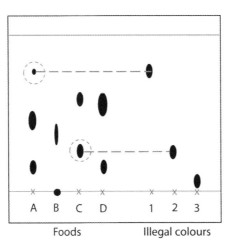

A B C D   1 2 3

Foods   Illegal colours

i) Food C produces a spot that travels the same distance as illegal colour 2. So it contains illegal colour 2.

ii) Food A has a very small spot that travels the same distance as illegal colour 1. So it contains a small amount of illegal colour 1.

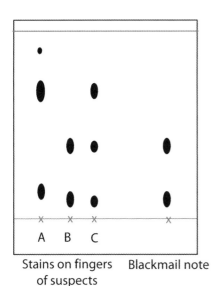

Stains on fingers   Blackmail note
of suspects

2 Police analysed the ink on a blackmail note. They compared it to stains from the fingers of three suspects.
The diagram shows the chromatogram.
Which suspect(s) might have written the note?
Explain your answer.

3 The diagram shows the results of chromatography on three different sauces:

- **A** is tomato and chilli
- **B** is tomato and pepper
- **C** is tomato and olive.

Sketch the chromatogram you would expect for a sauce that contains only tomato.

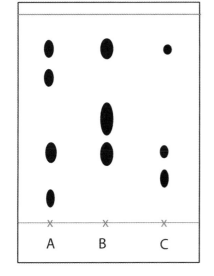

4 A historian wanted to discover the dye that ancient Egyptians used for their clothes.
The left chromatogram shows the results for the ancient dye.
The right one is for two dyes, madder and cochineal.
Does the ancient dye contain madder or cochineal? Explain your choice.

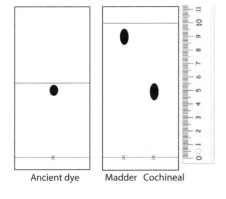

Ancient dye   Madder Cochineal

6.2 Separate two substances

1 The images show how you can make concentrated blackcurrant juice.

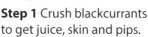

Step 1 Crush blackcurrants to get juice, skin and pips.

Step 2 Remove skin and pips.

Step 3 Make juice more concentrated.

Which separating technique could you use for **i)** Step 2 **ii)** Step 3?

Explain why each one works.

 Detect

I need to find properties that are different for each substance in the mixture.

 Recall

How do I decide which one to use?

Each technique works because of differences in properties:

1. Dissolving & filtering
Separates soluble from insoluble substances
Larger particles cannot fit through holes in filter paper
Smaller particles fit through holes in filter paper

2. Distilling
Higher boiling point substances

Lower boiling point liquid

4. Separating funnel
Liquid with lower density

Liquid with higher density (and which doesn't mix)

3. Evaporating
Lower boiling point liquid turns into vapour
Higher boiling point substances remain in evaporating dish

5. Paper chromatography
Separates different solutes in the same solution

 Solve

 What property differences did I use ?

Substance	Juice	Pips and skin	Water	Juice
Property	Particles in juice are small	Bits of solid are large	Solvent with lower boiling point	Solute with higher boiling point
Technique	Filtering		Evaporating	

i) Filtering works for step 2 because the particles in the liquid juice pass through the filter while the pips and skin stay in the paper.

ii) Evaporating works for step 3 because the water turns into vapour while the juice remain in the evaporating dish.

Your turn

2 These are the instructions for how to make beef stock.

Step 1 Mix beef bones, vegetables and water. Boil for 4 hours.

Step 2 Remove the bones and vegetables.

Step 3 Concentrate flavour by removing water.

Which separating techniques could you use for

i) Step 2 **ii)** Step 3? Explain why each one works.

3 Lavender oil is made by boiling lavender flowers in water.

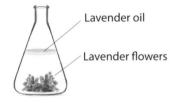

Lavender oil

Lavender flowers

Which separating technique could you use to:

i) Remove lavender flowers from the water.

ii) Remove lavender oil from the water.

Explain why you chose each technique using properties of the substances in the mixture.

4 Jo accidentally spilt salt into a beaker of water. Sam told her not to worry, as she can get the salt out using filtration.

i) Explain why Sam is wrong.

ii) Describe a technique that would remove the salt from the water.

6.3 Explain state changes

1 Naimah noticed that on a cold day her breath formed droplets of water on the inside of the car window. Explain this observation using the particle model.

 Detect

I need to think how forming water droplets links to the properties of particles.

 Recall

1. There is water vapour in the air. This is water in the gas state.
2. Forming water droplets is condensation, a change of state from gas to liquid.

> What happens to water vapour as it hits the window?

← Freezing   ← Condensing

	Solid	Liquid	Gas
Forces	Strong	Weaker	None. The particles move freely
Energy	Little	More. The energy partly overcomes the forces of attraction (but not enough to move freely)	Lots. The particles have enough energy to completely overcome the forces of attraction
Spac-ing	Very close together. Particles cannot change position	Close together. The particles move around each other	Far apart. The particles move in all directions

Melting →   Evaporating, or boiling →

3. A liquid evaporates at all temperatures. But it only boils at the boiling point.

 Solve

> What happens to particles when a gas cools?

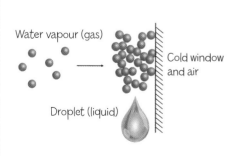

Water vapour (gas)

Cold window and air

Droplet (liquid)

The air contains water vapour, which is invisible. As the particles of water hit the cold window, they transfer some of their energy to it. With less energy, the particles can no longer overcome the forces of attraction pulling them together. They get closer together. In other words, water changes from a gas into the liquid state.

This is why there are droplets of water on the inside of the car window.

2 Megan found water droplets on her bedroom mirror on a winter morning. The condensation disappeared after she turned on the heater.
Explain what happened to the water droplets, using the particle model.

3 Samora noticed that the ice cubes in his drink get smaller and smaller.
Explain this observation using the particle model.

4 Josie did two experiments:
Experiment 1 Heating 200 g of ice until it melted.
Experiment 2 Heating 200 g of water up to 100 °C.
In each case, she measured the mass afterwards.
In which experiment did the mass change?
Explain why, using the particle model.

Experiment 1   **Experiment 2**

6.4 Changing states

1 The table shows the melting and boiling points of different substances.

Fill in the misssing column to show the states at room temperature.

Substance	Melting point (°C)	Boiling point (°C)	State at room temperature (21 °C)
Bromine	–7	59	
Chlorine	–101	–34	
Iodine	114	184	
Acetaldehyde	21	69	

 Detect

I need to work out if the substances are solid, liquids or gas at 21 °C.

Recall

What are the changes at melting and boiling points?

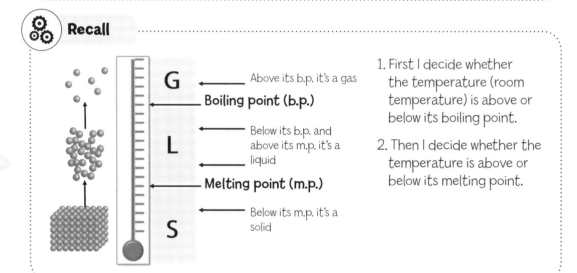

1. First I decide whether the temperature (room temperature) is above or below its boiling point.

2. Then I decide whether the temperature is above or below its melting point.

Solve

Why is bromine a liquid at 21°C?

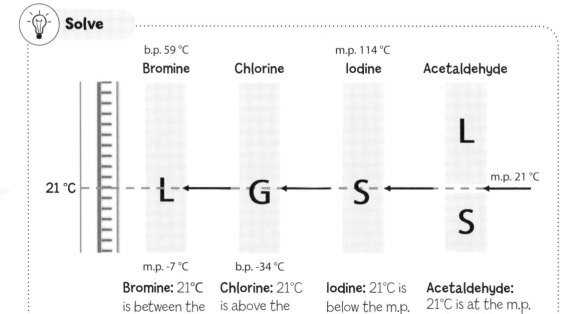

Bromine: 21°C is between the m.p. and b.p. so it is a liquid.

Chlorine: 21°C is above the b.p. so it is a gas.

Iodine: 21°C is below the m.p. so it is a solid.

Acetaldehyde: 21°C is at the m.p. so it could be a solid or liquid.

2 Methane is the main substance in natural gas. It has a melting point of -193 °C and a boiling point of -162 °C.

What is the state of methane at these temperatures:

i) - 194 °C   **ii)** −170 °C   **iii)** 160 °C?

3 Complete the table to show the state of each substance at 0°C.

Substance	Melting point (°C)	Boiling point (°C)	State at 0 °C
Bromine	−7	59	
Chlorine	−101	−34	
Iodine	114	184	
Acetaldehyde	21	69	
Formaldehyde	-21	-6	

4 The table gives the melting and boiling points of five substances.

Which substances are never liquid at the same temperature as substance B?

Explain your choices.

Substance	Melting point (°C)	Boiling point (°C)
A	-100	-100
B	-125	100
C	70	0
D	11	200
E	-80	-11

 **Example**

6.5 Solubility data

1 A student dissolves some ammonium bromide in water. The table shows how much dissolves at different temperatures.

Temperature (°C)	20	40	60
Solubility (g in 100g water)	75	90	105

i) At what temperature does 100 g of ammonium bromide fully dissolve?

A 20, 40 and 60 °C **B** 40 and 60 °C **C** 60°C only

ii) How much ammonium bromide would dissolve at 40 °C in 200 g of water?

 Detect

I need to think about how much solid dissolves in different amounts of water.

 Recall

Why is this pattern true?

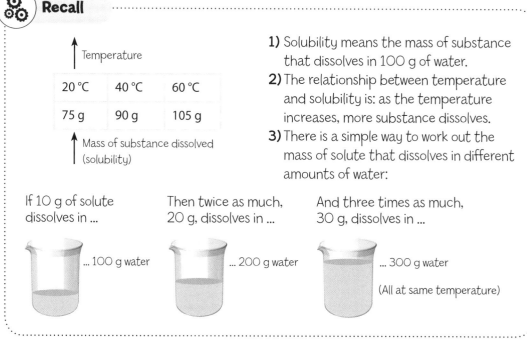

Temperature		
20 °C	40 °C	60 °C
75 g	90 g	105 g

Mass of substance dissolved (solubility)

1) Solubility means the mass of substance that dissolves in 100 g of water.

2) The relationship between temperature and solubility is: as the temperature increases, more substance dissolves.

3) There is a simple way to work out the mass of solute that dissolves in different amounts of water:

If 10 g of solute dissolves in ...
... 100 g water

Then twice as much, 20 g, dissolves in ...
... 200 g water

And three times as much, 30 g, dissolves in ...
... 300 g water
(All at same temperature)

Solve

Why does 90 g dissolve in 100 g of water?

i) At 20 °C and 40 °C, less than 100 g dissolves. At 60 °C, more than 100 g dissolves.

So the answer is C. 100 g only dissolves if the temperature is 60 °C.

ii) 200 g of water = twice as much as 100 g water. So twice as much ammonium bromide will dissolve.

We know 90 g solute dissolves in 100 g water at 40 °C , so...
90 x 2 = 180 g of ammonium bromide will dissolve in 200 g water.

Your turn

2 Sergei dissolves some potassium nitrate in 100 g of water. The table shows how much dissolves at different temperatures.

Temperature	10	20	30
Solubility (in 100g water)	24	35	48

i) At what temperature does 30 g potassium nitrate fully dissolve?

A 10, 20 and 30 °C   **B** 20 and 30 °C   **C** 30 °C only

ii) How much potassium nitrate would dissolve in 50 g of water at 10 °C ?

3 The table contains data about dissolving ammonia in 100 g of water at different temperatures.

Temperature (°C)	10	25	40
Solubility (g in 100g water)	70	50	35

i) At what temperature does 40 g of ammonia fully dissolve?

A 10 °C only   **B** 10 and 25 °C   **C** 10, 25 and 40 °C

ii) Mark prepares a litre of ammonia solution at 10 °C. How much ammonia can he dissolve?
1 litre of water has a mass of 1000g.

4 Paul investigated how a substance dissolves at different temperatures. The table shows his data.

Temperature (°C)	Solubility (g in 100g water)
20	20
40	24
60	29

Paul dissolved 15 g in 100 g of water at 40 °C.

How much more could he dissolve before the solution is saturated and no more dissolves?

1	/3	2	/3	3	/3	no hints: +1 Total	/10

6.6 Solubility curves

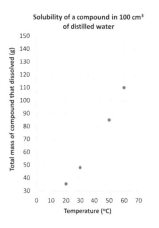

Solubility of a compound in 100 cm³ of distilled water

1 Luke added a substance to 100 cm³ of water at different temperatures. He plotted the amount dissolved at each temperature on a graph.

Estimate how many grams of the substance dissolve in 100 cm³ of water at 40 °C.

 Detect

I need to work out the amount dissolved for a temperature with no measurement.

 Recall

What does the relationship mean?

Most solid substances dissolve more easily at higher temperatures. The relationship usually takes the shape of a curve. To estimate how much dissolves at a particular temperature:

1. Draw a line of best fit through the points.
2. Find the temperature you want on the x axis.
3. Draw a vertical line from the temperature to the line of best fit.
4. Draw a horizontal line from the line to the y axis.
5. Read the value from the y axis.

 Solve

Why is my estimate a range?

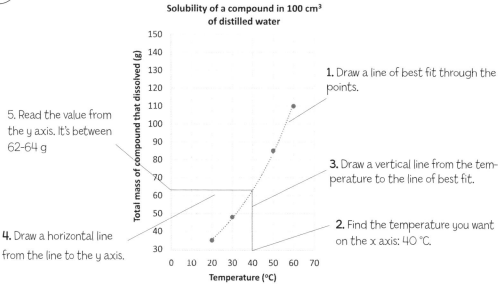

Solubility of a compound in 100 cm³ of distilled water

5. Read the value from the y axis. It's between 62-64 g

1. Draw a line of best fit through the points.

3. Draw a vertical line from the temperature to the line of best fit.

4. Draw a horizontal line from the line to the y axis.

2. Find the temperature you want on the x axis: 40 °C.

My estimate is that 62-64 g of the substance will dissolve at 40 °C.

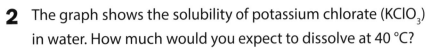

2 The graph shows the solubility of potassium chlorate ($KClO_3$) in water. How much would you expect to dissolve at 40 °C?

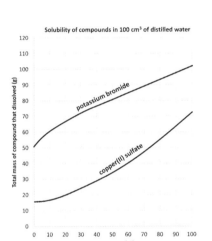

3 The graph shows the solubility of two substances.
   i) Estimate how much more copper (II) sulfate dissolves at 85 °C than at 20 °C.
   ii) Estimate how much less potassium bromide can be dissolved at 10 °C than at 30 °C.

4 The graph shows the solubility of two substances.
   i) At what temperature is their solubility the same?
   ii) Miri was able to dissolve 50 g of ammonium chloride in 100 g water.
   What is the lowest temperature the water could have been?

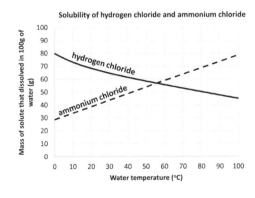

| 1 | /3 | 2 | /3 | 3 | /3 | no hints: +1 Total | /10 |

Practice

6.7 Mixed up problems

1 Ruth analysed an unknown food sample to see if it contained the dyes E133 and E102. The chromatogram shows her results.

Ruth concluded: *"The sample contains E133 and E102".*

Ahmed said: *"The sample contains only E133".*

Who do you agree with? Give a reason.

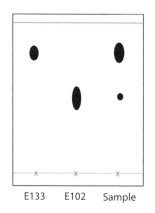

E133   E102   Sample

2 Brandy is an alcholic drink made from wine. The table compares the substances in brandy and wine.

Clive says you could change wine into brandy by gently warming to make the water evaporate.

i) Explain why this will not work

ii) Suggest a separating technique that will work.

	Wine	**Brandy**
Water	Large amount	Small amount
Alcohol (low boiling point)	12 %	50 %
Flavour substances (low boiling point)	Small amount	Large amount

3 Ruweida noticed that the puddle of water outside her house evaporated more quickly on warm days.

Explain this observation using the particle model.

1   /3   2   /3   3   /3   no hints: +1 Total   /10   © Mastery Science 2017

Practice

4 In cold weather, salt is added to roads to stop them becoming icy. The table shows properties of different salts that are used.

i) What can you conclude about the effect of adding salt on the freezing temperature?

ii) What happens to water with dissolved rock salt when the temperatures drops below -6.6 °C?

iii) Which salt could be used to stop water freezing when the temperature is -12 °C?

Type of salt added	Freezing temperature (°C)
No salt	0
Rock salt	-6.6
Potassium chloride	-11
Magnesium chloride	-15

5 Jeff investigated the solubility of different salts at 60 °C. Which salt, A, B, C or D, is most soluble?

Explain your choice.

Salt	Solubility at 60 °C
A	10g dissolve in 40g of water
B	20g dissolve in 100g of water
C	30g dissolve in 90g of water
D	40g dissolve in 80g of water

6 The graph shows the solubility of different substances in 100 g of water.

i) How much sodium nitrate dissolves at 10 °C?

ii) What is the lowest temperature that you can dissolve 80 g of potassium nitrate?

iii) At what temperature does 70 g of ammonia dissolve?

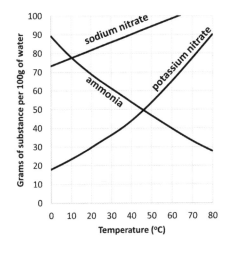

1	/3	2	/3	3	/3	no hints: +1 Total	/10

81

7.1 Functions of cell parts

1 The diagram shows a leaf infected with the tobacco mosaic virus (TMV).

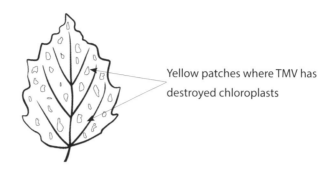

Yellow patches where TMV has destroyed chloroplasts

Explain how destroying chloroplasts will affect the growth of the plant.

 Detect

I need to think about the function of chloroplasts.

 Recall

> How is this cell part useful to the organism?

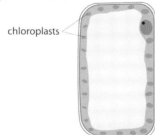

chloroplasts

1. Chloroplasts are green structures inside plant cells.
2. Their function is to carry out photosynthesis.
3. Photosynthesis is a process plants use to make food for themselves.
4. Growth is a life process. Organisms need food to grow.

 Solve

IF TMV destroys some of the chloroplasts,
THEN there will be fewer chloroplasts.

IF chloroplasts carry out photosynthesis
THEN fewer chloroplasts means less photosynthesis,

SO the plant will produce less food.
SO the plant will grow less.

OVERALL destroying chloroplasts will reduce the growth of the plant.

> How does this cell part affect growth?

2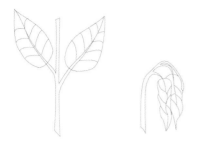

The diagram shows a plant wilting. This happens when plants cannot absorb enough water through their roots. Water moves out of the cell vacuole and the vacuole disappears. Explain why this causes the plant to wilt.

3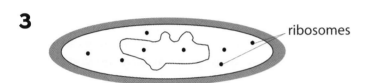

ribosomes

Antibiotics are drugs that kill bacteria. Some antibiotics stop ribosomes from working. Explain how this will kill a bacteria cell.

4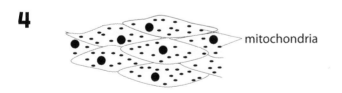

mitochondria

The diagram shows a group of muscle cells. Muscle cells have many more mitochondria than a typical animal cell. Explain why.

7.2 Using a microscope

1 This image of onion cells was taken with the microscope below.
How could you adjust the microscope to improve the image?

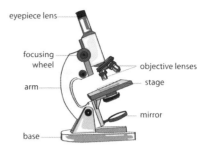

eyepiece lens

focusing wheel

arm

objective lenses

stage

mirror

base

 Detect

I need to think what is wrong with the image and how this relates to the microscope controls.

 Recall

What happens when you use a microscope?

How a microscope works:

4. The image is magnified again by the eyepiece lens.

3. The image is magnified by the objective lens, with a choice of magnification.

5. The image is focused by changing the distance between the specimen and the lenses.

2. Light travels through the specimen on the slide.

1. Light reflects off the mirror.

Start here

6. The total magnification is:

magnification of eyepiece lens **X** magnification of objective lens

 Solve

How did I deduce this?

IF the cells do not look sharp,
THEN the image is not in focus.

SO we can deduce that the lenses are the wrong distance from the specimen.

SO we should use the focusing wheel to move the lenses up or down until the image is in focus.

2

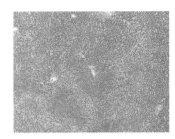

A scientist uses a light microscope to study human liver cells. The photograph shows what she sees. She wants to study the mitochondria in the cells.

Describe how she should adjust the microscope.

3

Rhys uses a light microscope to view some root cells. The image shows how he sets up the microscope. He has made a mistake. All he can see is a dark fuzzy circle.

Describe what Rhys should do to solve the problem.

4

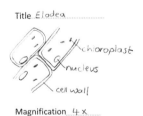

Title _Elodea_

chloroplast

nucleus

cell wall

Magnification _4 x_

Simran uses a light microscope to look at Elodea.

She uses an objective lens of 4X magnification. The eyepiece lens is 10X magnification.

Explain the mistake she has made on her drawing.

| 1 | /3 | 2 | /3 | 3 | /3 | no hints: +1 Total | /10 |

7.3 Identify cells

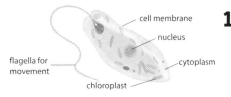

cell membrane
nucleus
flagella for movement
cytoplasm
chloroplast

1 The diagram shows a unicellular organism called Euglena. It lives in ponds and streams.

Is Euglena more like an animal or a plant cell? Give a reason.

 Detect

I need to compare the features of plant and animal cells to Euglena.

 Recall

What are the differences between animal and plant cells?

The are some parts that all cells share and some where animals, plants and bacteria are different (shaded).

Cell part	Animal ?	Plant ?	Bacteria ?
Cell membrane	✔	✔	✔
Cytoplasm	✔	✔	✔
Nucleus	✔	✔	X
Mitochondria	✔	✔	X
Ribosomes	✔	✔	✔
Chloroplasts	X	✔	X
Cell wall	X	✔	✔
Vacuole	X	✔	X

 Solve

Are Euglena's cell parts like animals or plants?

Cell part	Euglena?	Like?
Cell membrane	✔	All
Cytoplasm	✔	All
Nucleus	✔	Animal or plant
Chloroplasts	✔	Plant or bacteria
Cell wall	X	Animal
Vacuole	X	Animal or bacteria

Euglena does not have all the parts of an animal, plant or bacteria cell.
It does not have a cell wall like plant cells or bacteria. It does not have a vacuole like a plant. It has more parts of an animal cell than the other types. So it is more like an animal cell.

Your turn

2

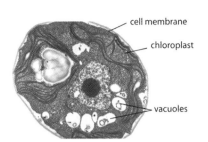

cell membrane
chloroplast
vacuoles

The microscope image shows a unicellular organism found in pond water. Some of its parts are labelled.
Is it an animal or plant cell? Give a reason for your choice.

3

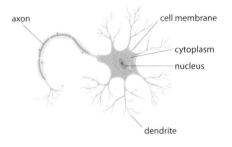

axon
cell membrane
cytoplasm
nucleus
dendrite

The diagram shows a type of cell.
Is it from a plant or animal? Give a reason for your choice.

4

Cell A   Cell B   Cell C

The diagram shows three types of cell.
Which one(s) could be plant cells?
Give a reason for your answer.

7.4 Functions of specialised cells

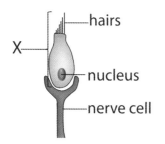

1 The diagram shows a specialised cell, X, from the human body.

When hairs at the top move, a signal is sent to the nerve cell.

i) What could the function of the cell be?

A To catch microbes

B To move nerve cells

C To detect sounds

ii) Explain your choice.

 Detect

I need to work out what the cell's adaptation is and what it does.

 Recall

What features of this cell are different to a typical cell?

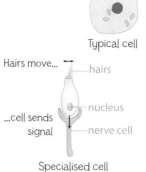

1. Identify the adaptation:
The specialised cell has hair cells that move.
A typical animal cell does not have hair cells.
So this is an adaptation.

2. Think about what the adaptation could do.
The specialised cell interacts with a nerve cell.
As the hairs move, it sends a signal to the nerve cell.
Nerve cells send signals to other parts of the body.

 Solve

How could the adaptation be used?

The cell has hairs that can move. The cell is also attached to a nerve cell that can detect the moving hairs and send a signal to the brain.

A is wrong because this adaptation wouldn't trap microbes.
B is wrong because nerve cells cannot move.

The answer is C.
It could work like this: sounds are vibrations in the air, which move the hairs. The movement sends a signal to the nerve cell. This is carried to the brain.

2

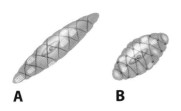

A   B

The image shows a type of animal cell that can exist in two states, A and B.

From which part of the body could this cell come?

A Bone

B Muscle

C Nerves

Explain your choice.

3

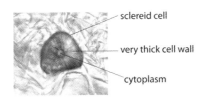

sclereid cell

very thick cell wall

cytoplasm

The microscope image shows a type of cell called a sclereid.

What could the function of a schlerid be?

A To absorb water

B To form the outer covering of seeds

C To produce food

Explain your choice.

4

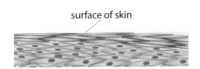

surface of skin

The image shows cells that form the top layer of the skin. They are tightly packed together.

Suggest the function of these cells. Give a reason.

1	/3	2	/3	3	/3	no hints: +1 Total	/10

7.5 How cells are specialised

1

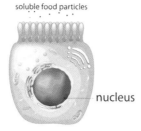

soluble food particles

nucleus

The diagram shows a human cell. Its function is to absorb soluble food particles.

Explain how it is adapted for this function.

 Detect

I need to work out what specialised feature the cell has and how this helps its job.

 Recall

What is an adaptation for?

1. The cell is different to a typical animal cell. The membrane is folded and has lots of long thin 'bits' sticking out.
2. Specialised cells are adapted for specific jobs:

Adaptation	Animal cell example	Plant cell example
Shape	Nerve cell	Root hair cell
	Long: to carry messages around the body	Increased surface area: to absorb more water
Missing parts	Red blood cell	Xylem cell
	No nucleus: to carry more oxygen	Hollow inside: to carry water up the stem
Extra parts	Sperm cell	Leaf cell
	Has a tail that moves: to swim to the egg	Has extra chloroplasts: to make food

 Solve

How are the human and root cells similar?

The membrane of this human cell is adapted. It is folded many times at the top. The cell is similar to a root hair cell. They are both long and thin and have a large surface area.

The root cell uses this adaptation to absorb more water. The human cell can use its large surface area to absorb food particles as they pass near.

Overall, the folds are an adaptation to give the cell a larger surface area so it can absorb food better.

2

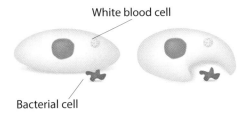

White blood cells destroy microorganisms that cause disease. The diagram shows what happens when a white blood cell meets a bacterial cell.

Explain how you think the white blood cell is adapted for its function.

3

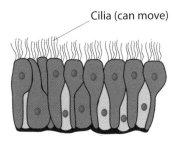

These cells are found inside the tubes that carry air to our lungs. They have cilia, which are like hairs that can move. The cells help to keep particles and microorganisms out of the lungs.

Explain how they are adapted for this function.

4

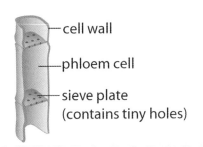

The diagram shows phloem cells in a plant stem. They stack on top of each other to form long tubes.

Their function is to carry sap, a sugary liquid, from the leaves to the rest of the plant.

Explain how phloem cells are adapted for this function.

Mixed up problems

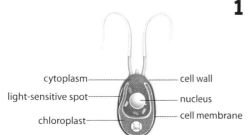

cytoplasm —
light-sensitive spot —
chloroplast —
— cell wall
— nucleus
— cell membrane

1 The diagram shows a unicellular organism called Chlamydomonas. It lives in pond water.
Which part of the cell could help it get food? Explain your answer.

2 Dinesh looks at cells down a microscope. The eyepiece lens has a magnification of 10X. The low power objective lens is 5X and the high power lens is 10X.
What is the total magnification of the cells that Dinesh views with the low power lens?

A 5X　　　　　**B** 15X　　　　**C** 50X　　　**D** 100X

3 The diagram shows a cell. It is not a plant or an animal cell. Explain why not.

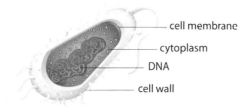

— cell membrane
— cytoplasm
— DNA
— cell wall

Practice

4 The image shows guard cells. They are found on the underside of a leaf where they surround a hole called a stoma. This lets gases enter and leave the leaf.
Suggest the function of guard cells. Give a reason.

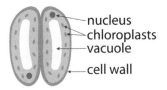

nucleus
chloroplasts
vacuole
cell wall

stoma

5 White blood cells destroy microorganisms that cause disease. The white blood cells need to travel to the site of infection. Use the diagram to explain one way that a white blood cell is adapted for this function.

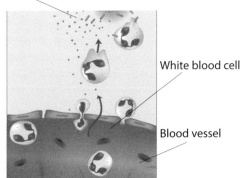

Microorganisms

White blood cell

Blood vessel

6 Pryesh is 7. He has a mitochondrial disease. Some of the mitochondria in his cells do not work.
Explain why he is shorter than his friends of the same age.

8.1 Interpret food webs

1

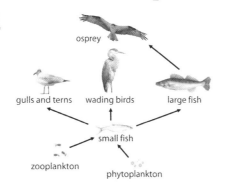

osprey

gulls and terns   wading birds   large fish

small fish

 zooplankton

 phytoplankton

The drawing shows part of a food web in a lake.

i) Why are phytoplankton found at the start of the food web?

ii) How does some of the energy from the phytoplankton end up in the osprey?

🔎 Detect

I need to work out how energy from phytoplankton gets passed to the osprey.

⚙️ Recall

What do the arrows in a food web show?

1. Food webs show how energy and material are transferred from organism to organism in a habitat.
2. The arrows in a food web show the direction of the energy transfer.

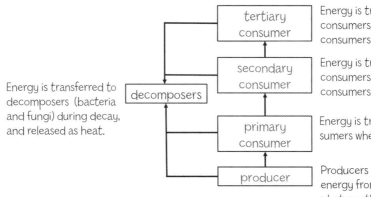

Energy is transferred to decomposers (bacteria and fungi) during decay, and released as heat.

Energy is transferred to tertiary consumers when they eat secondary consumers.

Energy is transferred to secondary consumers when they eat primary consumers.

Energy is transferred to primary consumers when they eat producers.

Producers (plants and algae) store energy from light in food during photosynthesis.

💡 Solve

How is the energy stored and transferred?

i) Phytoplankton use photosynthesis to store energy from sunlight in food. This energy can be passed to other organisms in the food web.

ii) The energy stored in phytoplankton is transferred up the food chain from one organism to another as its gets eaten by the one above it. Phytoplankton are eaten by primary consumers (small fish). Small fish are eaten by secondary consumers (big fish), which are eaten by the tertiary consumer (osprey).

2

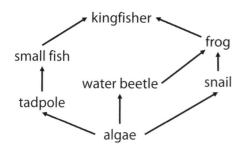

The drawing shows part of a food web in a river. Explain how some of the energy from the Sun ends up stored in a frog.

3

The temperature inside a pile of manure (animal waste) is higher than that of the surroundings. Explain why.

4 The energy stored in human tissues originally came from the Sun. Draw a diagram to explain why.

| 1 | /3 | 2 | /3 | 3 | /3 | no hints: +1 Total | /10 |

8.2 Change in population

1

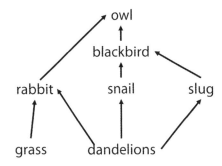

The drawing shows a grassland food web. Explain how an increase in the number of snails could cause an increase in the number of slugs.

 Detect

I need to use the food web to see how a change in one population affects another.

How does a population change affect the other organisms?

 Recall

If the population of an organism changes, it can affect the populations of the other organisms in the food chain.

this could happen

THEN there is more B for D to eat.
SO D eats fewer of C.

THEREFORE the population of C increases.

IF the population of organism B increases:

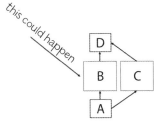

this could happen

THEN more A gets eaten.
SO there is less food for C.

THEREFORE the population of C decreases.

 Solve

Why is this true?

IF the population of snails increases,

THEN the blackbirds will have more snails to eat.

SO the blackbirds will eat fewer slugs.

THEREFORE the slug population will increase.

2

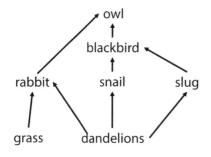

The diagram shows a grassland food web.

Explain how an increase in the number of snails could cause the number of slugs to decrease.

3

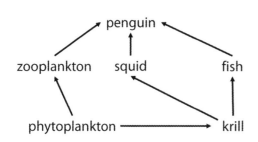

The diagram shows a food web in the Antarctic.

Explain how a decrease in the number of fish could result in the number of squid increasing.

4

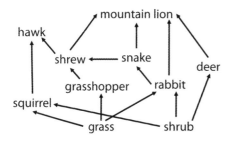

The diagram shows part of a food web in a mountain forest.

Explain why a decrease in the population of shrews might affect the hawks more than the mountain lions.

| 1 | /3 | 2 | /3 | 3 | /3 | no hints: +1 Total | /10 |

8.3 Explain resources

1

Scientists think dinosaurs went extinct when an asteroid impact covered the atmosphere in dust. The dust reduced the amount of light reaching the surface of the Earth.

Explain how these changes could have caused dinosaurs to become extinct.

 Detect

I need to think about how a lack of light could cause dinosaurs to die.

 Recall

What resources do organisms need?

1. Living organisms need resources to survive. They need these to grow and reproduce.
2. Organisms get their resources from their environment.

Resources that plants need	
Water (from soil) Light Carbon dioxide (from air or water)	To make food using photosynthesis
Minerals (from soil or water)	To build proteins for growth
Pollen	For reproduction
Warmth	

Resources that animals need	
Food (plants or other animals)	
Oxygen (from air or water)	
A mate	For reproduction
Warmth	
Shelter	For protection

 Solve

Plants are a resource that dinosaurs needed to provide their energy. Plants need light as their energy source, to make food using photosynthesis and grow.

Why did the dinosaur's energy source reduce?

Plant growth depends on how much sunlight plants receive. The asteroid impact reduced the amount of sunlight hitting the Earth. So there was less plant growth.

This meant that dinosaurs did not have enough food to eat, and died.

Your turn

2

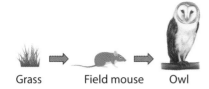

Grass   Field mouse   Owl

The diagram shows a food chain for a field.

Explain why the number of owls increases after a warm, wet summer.

3

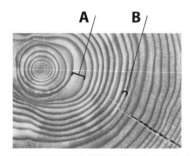

The diagram shows the rings in a tree trunk.

A ring is a layer of bark that grows around a tree trunk each year.

The more a tree grows that year, the thicker the ring.

Suggest reasons why ring A and ring B differ in thickness.

4

Cacti are plants that live in the desert. They have long roots which spread far away from the plant.

Explain how this helps the plant survive in the harsh desert climate.

| 1 | /3 | 2 | /3 | 3 | /3 | no hints: +1 Total | /10 |

 **Example**

8.4 Effect on population

1

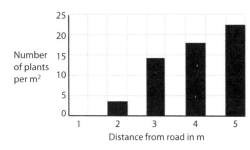

Number of plants per m² (y-axis: 0, 5, 10, 15, 20, 25)
Distance from road in m (x-axis: 1, 2, 3, 4, 5)

Fran counted the number of nettle plants near a busy road. The chart shows the results.

Explain one reason for the pattern she found.

 Detect

I need to describe and explain the change in the number of nettle plants.

How do factors affect populations?

 Recall

1. Plant and animal numbers (population) are affected by different factors.
2. Living factors (biotic) are other animals and plants, disease etc.
3. Non living factors (abiotic) are light, water, minerals, temperature, pollution etc.

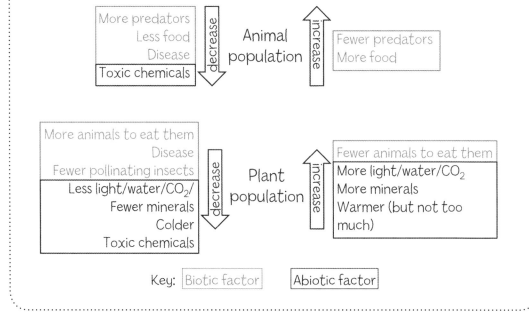

More predators
Less food
Disease
Toxic chemicals
→ decrease ← Animal population → increase ← Fewer predators / More food

More animals to eat them
Disease
Fewer pollinating insects
Less light/water/CO_2/
Fewer minerals
Colder
Toxic chemicals
→ decrease ← Plant population → increase ← Fewer animals to eat them / More light/water/CO_2 / More minerals / Warmer (but not too much)

Key: Biotic factor   Abiotic factor

 Solve

b) Why are distance from the road and population linked?

The pattern is that the number of plants increases as you move further away from the road. Vehicles produce polluting gases from their exhausts. The bigger the distance from the road, the less pollution there is.

Some of the gases are toxic chemicals. These are an abiotic factor that decreases a plant population. This explains the pattern: the bigger the distance from the road, the lower the amount of toxic chemicals, and the more the plants could grow.

Your turn

2

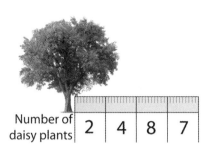

Number of daisy plants	2	4	8	7

Frida counted the number of daisies growing at different distances from a tree, by laying a tape measure on the ground. The diagram shows her results.

Suggest an explanation for the pattern Frida found.

3

Butterflies lay their eggs on the leaves of plants. Caterpillars hatch from the eggs.

What will happen to the population of butterflies if the number of plants decreases?

4

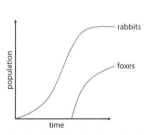

Foxes are predators of rabbits. The graph shows how the numbers of rabbits and foxes in a habitat change over time.

Suggest an explanation for the pattern.

8.5 Explain competition

1 When the seedpods of the lupin plant dry out, its seeds are sent flying out. They will eventually grow into offspring. Explain how this mechanism helps the parent and offspring plants to grow successfully.

Detect

I need to think why there needs to be distance between parent and offspring plants.

What is competition?

Recall

Organisms

Resources

1. Plants and animals compete for the resources they need to grow - light, water, food, space and minerals.
2. Organisms that live in the same area have to share resources. There are not enough resources for all of them, so they compete - like musical chairs.

Like the players who get the chairs, the organisms best at competition get enough resources to survive and grow.

Just as players without a chair are out, organisms that do not get enough resources die.

Increasing access to resources is like adding more chairs, and means more organisms can thrive.

Solve

The lupin plants need resources like light, minerals and water to grow and survive so they can reproduce.

Why is there less competition?

If the parent and the offspring live in the same area, they will compete for the resources there. Spreading the seeds far away from the parent plant means that the offspring have access to more resources. This reduces the competition. So the lupin plants will grow more, and more of them will survive.

Your turn

2

The image shows a farmer spraying a herbicide onto his field of soy plants. This kills any weeds.
Explain why removing weeds increases the growth of the soy plants.

3

Cheetahs are predators of animals such as deer. In a population of cheetahs, some are faster than others.
Explain why the faster cheetahs have a higher chance of survival.

4

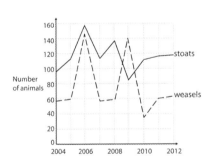

Stoats and weasels are wild animals that both eat rabbits. The graph shows how the numbers of animals living in the same area have changed between 2004 and 2012. Suggest why the numbers of weasels changed between 2008 and 2010.

| 1 | /3 | 2 | /3 | 3 | /3 | no hints: +1 Total | /10 |

Mixed up problems

1 The drawing shows part of a food web in a field.
Explain how some of the energy from the Sun ends up stored in a owl.

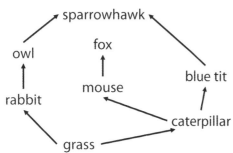

2 The diagram shows a food web.
Explain how a decrease in the population of snakes could affect the population of:
i) Kites
ii) Owls.

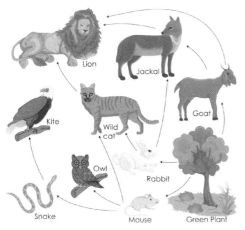

3 Fertilisers contain minerals.
Explain why farmers add fertilisers to the soil in which their crops grow.

Practice

4 Hawks are predators of mice. The table shows the results scientists collected for the population of hawks and mice in an area.

Describe how the population of hawks changes and explain why.

Year	Number of mice	Number of hawks
2002	205	23
2004	201	25
2005	145	23
2006	122	18
2007	112	14
2008	109	11

5 Rhododendron plants produce a poisonous chemical from their roots, which enters the soil.
Explain how this enables rhododendron plants to grow bigger and faster than other plants.

6 This food web is from a lake. There is heavy metal pollution in the lake.
Explain why it is not safe for humans to eat the large fish in the lake.

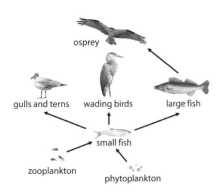

| 1 | /3 | 2 | /3 | 3 | /3 | no hints: +1 Total | /10 |

9.1 Sexual vs asexual

1 Milo is a Labradoodle. His mother has curly brown fur. His father has straight black fur. Milo has curly black fur. Explain why Milo has these two characteristics.

Father: Labrador   Mother: Poodle   Milo: Labradoodle

 Detect

I need to work out why Milo looks a bit like each of his parents.

 Recall

1. There are two different kinds of reproduction: sexual and asexual.
2. Most animals use sexual. Many plants use a mixture. Most single-cell organisms (like bacteria) use asexual.

> Sexual/ asexual – what's the difference?

Type	Number of parents	What happens	Genetic material in the offspring
Asexual	1	The parent cell copies itself to produce offspring. parent cell → nucleus divides → cytoplasm divides → two daughter cells	Same as parent. So it gets all its parent's characteristics.
Sexual	2	female gamete → fertilisation → embryo; Nucleus contains genetic material; zygote; cells are copied; male gamete. In plants, gametes are in pollen (male) and the ovule (female).	Mixture from both parents. So some characteristics will be the same as one parent's, and some the same as the other's.

 Solve

> How does this explain what happened?

Milo was produced by sexual reproduction. During fertilisation, genetic material from his mother's egg was combined with genetic material from his father's sperm.

So, he has characteristics from both his mother and his father.

The characteristic Milo shares with his mother is curly fur. The characteristic Milo shares with his father is black fur.

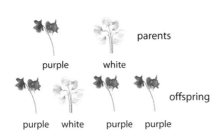

purple   white   parents

purple   white   purple   purple   offspring

2 A scientist bred two pea plants together. One had white flowers with and the other purple flowers. Some of the offspring had white flowers and some had purple flowers. Explain why the offspring had a mixture of colours.

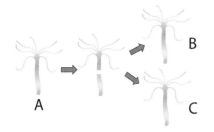

A   B   C

3 The diagram shows how hydra reproduce.
i) Describe how the characteristics of hydra A, B and C compare
ii) Explain your answer to i) in terms of the different types of reproduction.

4 Liz and Tim want a baby. However, Liz cannot produce any eggs. Her friend Kerry donates an egg. It is fertilised in a dish with Tim's sperm. Then it is placed in Liz's uterus to grow.
Which two people will the baby share characteristics with? Explain your answer.

| 1 | /3 | 2 | /3 | 3 | /3 | no hints: +1 Total | /10 |

9.2 Reproductive organs

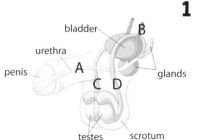

bladder
urethra
penis
A
B
C D
glands
testes
scrotum

1 A vasectomy is a procedure to prevent fertilisation by removing sperm from the semen. The doctor cuts tubes in the male reproductive system and seals the ends.
Which two letters show where the doctor should cut?

 Detect

I need to know the journey sperm makes from the man to the egg in the woman.

 Recall

A sperm has to meet an egg to fertilise it:

What does each part of the reproductive system do?

What happens inside a man	
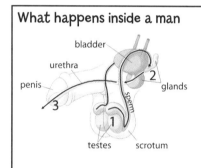 bladder urethra penis glands 2 sperm 3 1 testes scrotum	**1.** Testes produce sperm, which travels through tubes to the penis. **2.** Liquid from glands is added to the sperm to make semen. **3.** In sexual intercourse, semen containing millions of sperm is released from the penis into the woman's vagina.
What happens inside a woman	
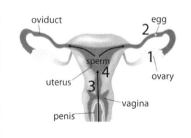 oviduct egg 2 sperm 4 1 uterus 3 ovary vagina penis	**4.** Once a month, an egg is released from one ovary. **5.** The egg travels down the oviduct towards the uterus. **6.** If sexual intercourse takes place, the sperm swim towards the oviducts. This is a difficult journey. Not many sperm will complete it. **7.** If a sperm does meet an egg, it fertilises it. **8.** The fertilised egg settles into the uterus lining where it develops into a foetus.

 Solve

Where are the sperm made?

The doctor needs to stop the semen from containing sperm.

If tube C is cut, it stops sperm from one testis. If tube D is cut, it stops sperm from the other.

So both tubes C and D need to be cut.

Your turn

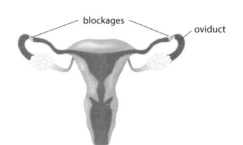

2 Mira has a blockage in both her oviducts. The diagram shows the positions of the blockages.

Explain how these blockages might affect her becoming pregnant.

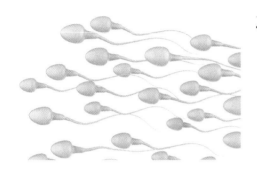

3 During sexual intercourse, the man releases 250 million sperm into the woman's vagina.

Explain why it is necessary to release so many sperm.

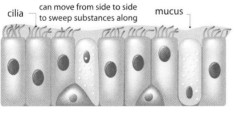

4 The diagram shows cells that line the oviducts. One kind makes sticky mucus and the other kind has cilia on its surface. Suggest how these two types of cell help fertilisation to take place.

9.3 Menstrual cycle

1 The graph shows how the lining of the uterus changes in thickness over a 28 day cycle. Explain the change in the uterus lining between days 1 and 5.

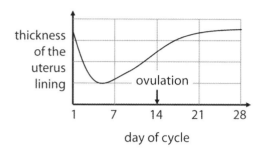

 Detect

I need to think about why the lining of the uterus changes during the menstrual cycle.

 Recall

What happens from day 1-5 of the menstrual cycle?

The thickness of the uterus lining changes during the 28 day menstrual cycle. It is linked to these stages:

Stage 4: The uterus lining continues to thicken. If the egg is fertilised, it settles into the lining and grows into a foetus. If not, the cycle starts again.

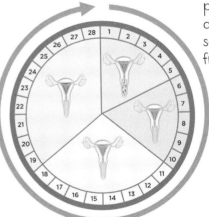

Stage 1: Menstruation (the period). The lining breaks down and leaves the body, so it can be replaced by a fresh one.

Stage 2: The uterus lining is replaced and starts to thicken.

Stage 3: Ovulation. An egg is released from an ovary. This normally happens around day 14.

 Solve

Why is the uterus lining getting thinner?

The graph shows the thickness of the uterus lining decreasing a lot during days 1-5. This is the time in the menstrual cycle when menstruation occurs. In this process, the uterus lining breaks down.

So it is menstruation that causes the change in the uterus lining during days 1-15.

Your turn

2 The diagram shows how the thickness of the uterus lining changes over 28 days. Give a reason for the change in thickness between days 14 and 28.

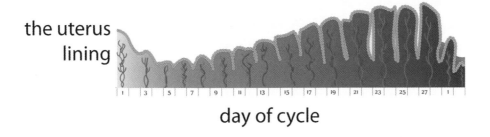

day of cycle

3 The diagram shows the female reproductive organs during the menstrual cycle. Which letter shows the position of the egg on day 18?
Explain your choice.

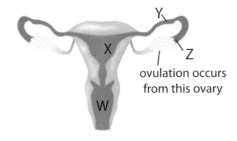

ovulation occurs from this ovary

4 The diagram shows how the thickness of the uterus lining changes during the menstrual cycle. Which letter represents day 24?

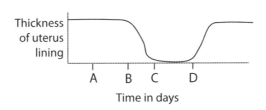

Time in days

| 1 | /3 | 2 | /3 | 3 | /3 | no hints: +1 Total | /10 |

9.4 Pregnancy time

1 Jana ovulates on day 14 of her menstrual cycle. She wants to get pregnant. An egg survives 1 day after ovulation. Sperm survive for up to 5 days inside the woman's reproductive system.

On which days would sexual intercourse allow her to get pregnant?

 Detect

I need to work out on which dates it is possible for an egg and sperm to meet.

 Recall

1. The egg goes through different stages in the 28 day menstrual cycle.
2. The live egg and sperm have to meet for fertilisation to happen.
3. Ovulation usually occurs in the middle of the cycle.
4. Not all women's cycles are exactly the same (and they can change month to month).

When is the egg alive?

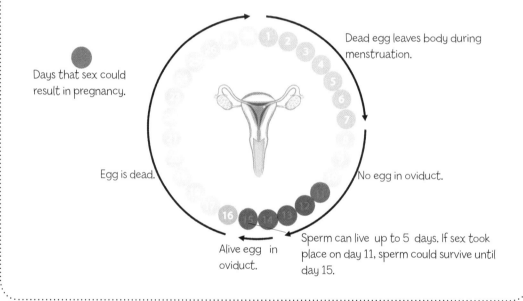

Days that sex could result in pregnancy.

Dead egg leaves body during menstruation.

Egg is dead.

No egg in oviduct.

Alive egg in oviduct.

Sperm can live up to 5 days. If sex took place on day 11, sperm could survive until day 15.

 Solve

Jana's ovulation happens on day 14. The egg would be alive until day 15. After this date, the egg would be dead and fertilisation could not take place.

Why is the range only 5 days?

Sperm can survive for up to 5 days. So if sex took place on day 11, the sperm would still be alive 5 days later - on day 15 - to fertilise the egg. This is the latest day sex could result in pregnancy.

So Jana could get pregnant if sexual intercourse took place between days 11 and 15.

Your turn

2 A woman wants to become pregnant. She knows that she will next ovulate on May 25th.
On which days should she have sexual intercourse in order to become pregnant?

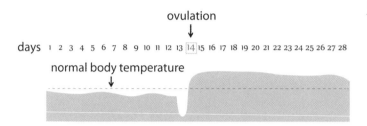

3 The graph shows how body temperature changes during the menstrual cycle. Explain how measuring body temperature could help a woman who wants to become pregnant.

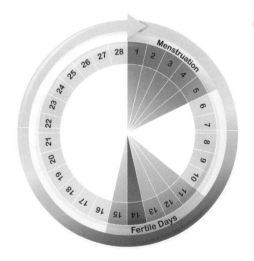

4 The diagram shows how a woman's fertility changes throughout the menstrual cycle.
Explain why the woman is probably infertile on days 16-28.

 **Example**

9.5 Supporting the foetus

1 A human pregnancy lasts around 40 weeks. During this time, the foetus grows and becomes heavier. The placenta also increases in size during pregnancy. Give an explanation for the change in the placenta.

 Detect

I need to think about the function of the placenta during pregnancy.

 Recall

How does the placenta support the baby?

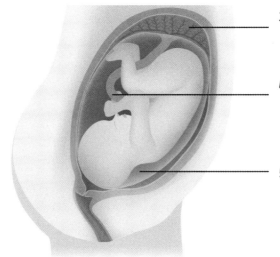

1. A foetus grows inside its mother's uterus.

2. The foetus grows by making new cells. It needs oxygen and food from the mother. It also needs to get rid of poisonous waste.

3. The placenta has lots of blood vessels. They carry substances between the mother and the foetus.

4. The umbilical cord also contains blood vessels. They carry substances between the placenta and the foetus.

5. The amniotic fluid is a liquid. It acts like a cushion, to protect the foetus from bumps and knocks.

 Solve

Why does the foetus need more substances?

As the foetus grows, it makes new cells. So it needs more food and oxygen. The foetus also needs to remove more waste.

So the placenta needs to be bigger, with more blood vessels, in order carry more substances between the mother and foetus.

This is why, as the foetus grows, the placenta also needs to grow.

Your turn

2 Twins usually have a much lower mass at birth than babies from single pregnancies. In most cases, identical twins in the uterus share a single placenta.
Explain why twins have a lower birth mass than single babies.

3 During pregnancy, a woman's heart has to pump more blood around the body.
Suggest why this is.

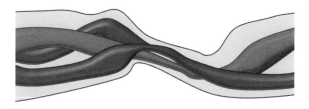

4 The diagram shows how the umbilical cord can become squashed during birth.
Explain why it is important that the baby is born quickly if this happens.

| 1 | /3 | 2 | /3 | 3 | /3 | no hints: +1 Total | /10 |

Mixed up problems

1 Sam has a spider plant in his house. He notices that small plants start growing on the parent plant.
They look identical to each other and the parent.
Suggest what type of reproduction has happened. Give a reason.

2 Some men produce sperm with shorter tails than normal.
Explain how this could affect fertilisation.

normal   tail defect

3 The diagram shows how the thickness of the uterus lining changes during the menstrual cycle.
Which letter represents menstruation happening? Explain your choice.

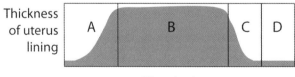

Thickness of uterus lining

A   B   C   D

Time in days

1   /3   2   /3   3   /3   no hints: +1 Total   /10

4 One method to avoid becoming pregnant is to have sexual intercourse only on days in the menstrual cycle when the woman is infertile.

Explain why this method is not very reliable.

5 Tobacco smoke contains the gas carbon monoxide.

The gas reduces the amount of oxygen carried in the blood.

Explain why babies whose mothers smoked in pregnancy may be born weighing less than normal.

6 Algae can reproduce sexually and asexually. The boxes show two stages of reproduction. Offspring from stage 2 have some characteristics that are the same as alga A and some that are different. Explain why this is.

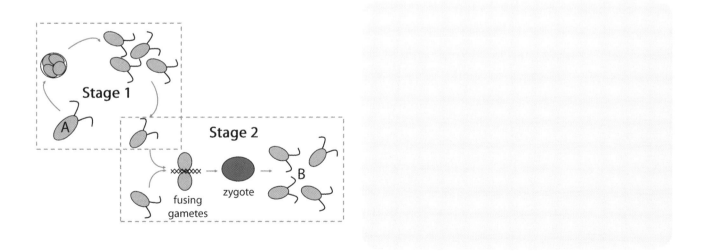

1	/3	2	/3	3	/3	no hints: +1 Total	/10

 **Oops**

Answers p.134

10.1 Watch out !

1 The reindeer pulls Santa's sleigh on the ground with a force of 2000 N. The sleigh does not move.

2000 N

What is the force of friction from the ground?

A 0 N   **B** 2000 N   **C** More than 2000 N

 Detect

The question tells me one force and I need to work out the other one.

Is this correct? Why?

 Recall

1. The force of friction acts in the opposite direction to the pull - to the left.
2. When an object is not moving, or it moves at steady speed, the forces on it are balanced.

What's wrong with this reason?

 Solve

The answer is C.   **X It's B.**
This is because friction 'wins' against the pulling force.

**Friction is never greater than the force it is opposing.
The forces are balanced, so the friction is equal and opposite to the pull – 2000 N.**

Your turn

2 Terri uses a pulley to lift a weight. The tension in the rope that pulls up the weight is 20 N. The weight moves upwards at a constant speed.
What is the weight Terri is lifting? Give a reason for your choice.

A 0 N   **B** Less than 20 N   **C** 20 N

 **20 N**

© Mastery Science 2017

10.2 Watch out !

1 Rafi built these circuits. Decide whether the bulb in each circuit is on or off.
Give a reason for your choices.

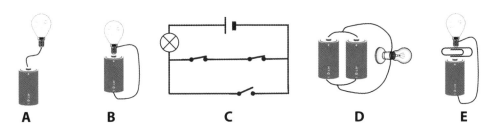

A   B   C   D   E

 Detect ....

I need to work out if current can flow in each circuit.

 **Recall** ....

Did I miss
out anything
important?

1. Current flows from one terminal of the battery to the other.
2. Current flows if there is a complete circuit.

 Solve ....

What didn't I
understand?

Circuit	Bulb	Reason
A	On	The bulb is touching the battery
B	Off	The circuit is not complete
C	Off	One of the switches is open
D	Off	The batteries cancel out
E	Off	There is a gap because of the paper clip

X It's off. Only one terminal is connected

X It's on. Both terminals of the bulb and battery are connected

X It's on. The closed switch makes one complete loop

X It's on. The batteries push current the same way

X It's on. There is a complete circuit through the metal

2 Ed built these circuits. In which ones do the bulbs light? Give a reason.

 Your turn

A   B   C   D   E

 **Oops**

10.3 Watch out !

1 A cricket ball is dropped.

What happens to the energy in its kinetic energy (KE) and gravitational potential energy (GPE) stores?

A Both KE and GPE increase

B Both KE and GPE decrease

C KE decreases and GPE increases

D KE increases and GPE decreases

Explain your choice.

 Detect

I need to know how KE and GPE change when an object falls.

 Recall

Is 2 correct? Why?

1. As an object falls, energy moves from one store to another. No energy is lost or gained.
2. KE depends on speed. The ball gets faster as it loses height.
3. GPE depends on height. The ball loses height as it falls.

 Solve

What's wrong with this reason?

The answer is B. This because some energy is always wasted. So the energies must decrease.

X It's D. At the top it has GPE and zero KE. Energy in the GPE store decreases as the ball loses height. The energy moves to the KE store. So KE increases.

Your turn

2 Jemma does the high jump. Which answer best describes the energy change from the bottom to the top of her jump?

A The total energy increases

B The total energy decreases

C Energy in the GPE store reduces

D Energy in the KE store reduces

Explain your choice.

10.4 Watch out !

1 Deep 'weighs' his toy astronaut using a pair of scales and a force meter.

The diagrams give the readings.

Pair of scales reading = 0.2 kg

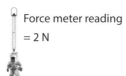 Force meter reading = 2 N

Imagine he repeats the experiment on the Moon.

Which answer shows how the readings change?

	Pair of scales reading on Moon	Forcemeter reading on Moon
A	Less	Less
B	Same	Less
C	Less	Same
D	Same	Same

 Detect

I need to decide if mass and weight are the same or different on the Moon.

 Recall

Is this correct? Why?

1. Mass is measured in kg.
2. Weight is a force and is measured in N.
3. The Moon has less gravity than Earth. So the toy weighs less on the Moon.

 Solve

What's wrong with this reason?

The answer is A. It's because the mass decreases as well as the weight.

X It's B. Weight and mass aren't the same. Weight is the force due to gravity. It changes on another planet. Mass is the amount of stuff. It stays the same everywhere.

2 An astronaut finds that she can jump much higher on the Moon than on Earth.

What is the best explanation for this? Give a reason for your choice.

A There is no air resistance on the Moon to slow her down

B There is less air resistance on the Moon to slow her down

C Her mass is less on the Moon and so she jumps higher

D Her weight is less on the Moon because there is less gravity

 Your turn

10.5 Watch out !

1 Bobbie mixed some table salt with some water. It made brine.

Is this a chemical change or a physical change?
Explain your answer.

 Detect

I need to decide if the two substances combined to make a new substance.

Is this correct? Why?

 Recall

1. Salt dissolves in water.
2. Forming a new substance is a sign of chemical change.

What's wrong with this reason?

 Solve

It's a chemical change.
This is because a new substance has formed.

X It's a physical change. Adding salt to water only makes a mixture of the two substances – salt and water (brine means very salty water). The salt dissolves but does not form a new substance.

Your turn

2 Rupert added some dark red beetroot juice to water. The liquid turned pink.
Is this a chemical change or a physical change? Explain your answer.

10.6 Watch out !

1 The graph shows the mass of hydrogen chloride and ammonium chloride that dissolve in 100 g of water at different temperatures.

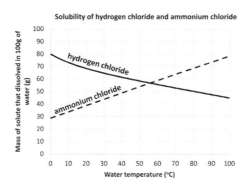

How much hydrogen chloride dissolves in 50 g of water at 75 °C?

A 50 g

B 25 g

C 64 g

D 32 g

 Detect

I need to work out how much dissolves from the graph.

 Recall

Is this correct? Why?

1. Draw a line of best fit through the points.
2. Find the temperature you want on the x axis.
3. Draw a vertical line from the temperature to the line of best fit.
4. Draw a horizontal line from the line of best fit to the y axis.
5. Read the value from the y axis.

 Solve

What did I do wrong?

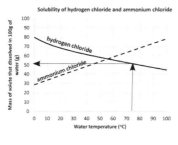

When I draw a line up from 75 °C, it meets the hydrogen chloride curve at 50 g (on the y axis).

So the answer is A: 50 g.

X it's B: 25 g. True, 50 g of hydrogen chloride dissolves in 100g of water. The question says there is 50g of water. So we have to halve the amount: 25 g dissolves in 50 g of water.

Your turn

2 The table shows how much of a substance X, dissolves in 100g of water at different temperatures.

Predict the mass of substance X that dissolves in 200 g of water at 50 °C.

Temperature (°C)	20	40	60
Solubility (g in100 g water)	70	90	110

10.7 Watch out !

1 The diagram shows a cell.

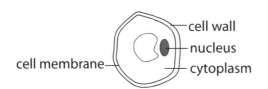

cell wall
nucleus
cytoplasm
cell membrane

What type of cell is it?

A Animal

B Bacteria

C Plant

Give a reason for your choice.

 Detect

I need to compare the features of the cell with those of an animal, bacteria and plant cell.

 Recall

Is this correct? Why?

1. Bacteria cells do not have a nucleus.
2. Plant cells have chloroplasts.

 Solve

What's wrong with this reason?

The answer is A.
The cell has a nucleus so it isn't a bacteria cell. It doesn't have any chloroplasts so it isn't a plant cell. It must be an animal cell.

X It's C. It isn't an animal cell because it has a cell wall. It isn't a bacteria cell because it has a nucleus. It must be a plant cell. Not all plant cells have chloroplasts – root cells don't.

Your turn

2 The diagram shows a cell with some of the parts labelled.

What type of cell is it?

A Animal   **B** Bacteria   **C** Plant

Give a reason for your choice.

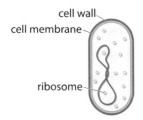

cell wall
cell membrane
ribosome

 **Oops**

10.8 Watch out !

1 The diagram shows part of a food web.

Predict what will happen to the population of carrots if the population of grasses decreases.

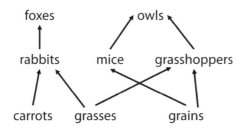

foxes → owls

rabbits   mice   grasshoppers

carrots   grasses   grains

 Detect

I need to work out how a change in one population could affect another.

 Recall

Is this correct. Why?

1. The food chain shows the feeding relationship between producers and consumers.
2. Carrots and grasses are both producers. They are eaten by consumers (rabbits and grasshoppers).

 Solve

What's wrong with the answer?

The answer is that the population of carrots will not change if the population of grasses decreases. This is because they are both producers. They are not linked by arrows. Neither eats the other one.

X The population of carrots will decrease. Changes can affect organisms that are not directly linked: rabbits eat both carrots and grasses. Less grass means the rabbits have to eat more carrots.

2 In the food web from question 1, what will happen to the population of owls if there are fewer grains?

Give a reason for your answer.

Your turn

10.9 Watch out !

1 The diagram shows how the thickness of a woman's uterus changes over a month.

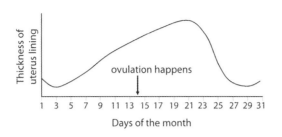

Days of the month

Between which days should sexual intercourse take place for her to become pregnant?

A Days 3-7

B Days 11-15

C Days 21-27

D Days 27-31

 Detect

I need to relate the thickness of the uterus lining to what happens in fertilisation.

Is this correct? Why?

 Recall

1. To get pregnant, there must be fertilisation - an egg meets a sperm.
2. The uterus lining has to be thick for a woman to get pregnant. This is because the embryo settles into the lining before it develops.

What's wrong with this reason?

 Solve

The answer is C - days 21-27.
This is because day 21 is the time in the month when the lining is the thickest.

X The answer is B – days 11-15. Sexual intercourse has to happen a few days before or after ovulation so fertilisation takes place. Between days 21-27 is menstruation, when the dead egg is removed from the body.

Your turn

2 A woman ovulates on 11th February.

Estimate the day in February when her menstruation is likely to start.

Hints

Contact Forces

3.1 Find missing forces
Q2. Write down the total force upwards and downwards.
Q3. Write down the total force left and right.
Q4. Write down the total force upwards and downwards.

3.2 Explain floating & sinking
Q2. How does removing mass affect density?
Q3. Try putting the densities in order.
Q4. Think why the balloon sinks in air.

3.3 Calculate density
Q2. What is the meaning of a high density?
Q3. Remember the formula for density.
Q4. How does volume affect density?

3.4 Friction factors
Q2. How much does the force change each time?
Q3. Which shows friction doubles when weight doubles?
Q4. What other factors could affect friction and the results?

3.5 Friction and motion
Q2. How does air resistance change as she speeds up?
Q3. How does drag change as the ball gets faster?
Q4. When are the weight and air resistance balanced?

3.6 Mixed up problems
Q1. What is the total upwards force to balance weight?
Q2. Remember the formula for density.
Q3. Try putting the densities in order.
Q4. How will friction change for the same weight?
Q5. Is the force to move the trainer exactly 2.5 or 3 N?
Q6. What is air resistance on the Moon?

Electric circuits

2.1 Complete loops
Q2. How many bulbs are in the loop of switch D?
Q3. Are the heater and fan in the same loop?
Q4. Which loops are complete with this combination?

2.2 Ammeter readings
Q2. i) How do you combine several loops?
Q3. i) A1 + A2 = A3. ii) What happens to current when you add more components?
Q4. What do you know about current in a loop?

2.3 Bulb brightness
Q2. Which circuit has more components?
Q3. Which loops combine?
Q4. Which loop has more components?

2.4 Batteries to bulbs
Q2. The resistors are like bulbs, compare it to Q1.
Q3. i)-iii) Think about the number of batteries per bulb.
Q4. What is the effect of cancelling out two batteries?

2.5 Mixed up problems
Q1. Where can the switch be part of both loops?
Q2. Remember how the currents from each loop combine.
Q3. Is it position or resistance that affects brightness?
Q4. Think about the number of batteries per bulb.
Q5. Which loops are complete when switch Z is open?
Q6. How do the currents in the three loops combine?

Energy transfer

3.1 Identify energy change
Q2. Which stores are filled before the catapult fires?
Q3. How much bigger is the input than output store?
Q4. What energy store does the fuel (gas) have?

3.2 Energy in/out
Q2. First calculate the energy in two mastery bars.
Q3. i) Look at the value with skim milk. ii) Put the answer from i) into the equation: energy in = energy out.
Q4. Find the total energy for both activities. See how much energy is left from two servings of cereal.

3.3 KE and GPE transfers
Q2. i) How much GPE has the marble lost when it is half way down? ii) What has happened to the GPE at C?
Q3. i)-iii) KE is biggest when the speed is fastest. GPE is biggest when the height is greatest.
Q4. i)-iv) KE is biggest when the speed is fastest. GPE is biggest when the height is greatest.

3.4 Temperature change
Q2. What is the average of the hot and cold buckets?
Q3. Will the temperature be closer to the 100 g or 200 g?
Q4. Is the final temperature closer to the tea or cold water?

3.5 Temperature graphs
Q2. The line for the beaker that warms quicker is steeper.
Q3. Start by drawing a dotted line 'if no milk added'. Adding milk makes the temperature drop quickly.
Q4. The line for the one that cools quicker has a steeper slope.

3.6 Interpret energy diagrams
Q2. How many squares are there at the start?
Q3. What store does the energy move to when a car brakes?
Q4. What device uses a chemical energy store?

3.7 Identify wasted energy
Q2. i)-ii) What input energy store does a tablet use? Which stores are part of watching a cartoon and which not?
Q3. i)-ii) Energy is wasted where there is friction.
Q4. The height relates to the gravitational potential energy.

3.8 Calculate efficiency
Q2. i) What fraction of energy is transferred to a useful store? ii) The KE is the efficiency x the amount of input energy.
Q3. What fraction of energy is transferred to a useful store?
Q4. What fraction of energy is transferred to a useful store?

3.9 Mixed up problems
Q1. What is the input energy store and the final output store?
Q2. Calculate how much energy for 100 minutes of standing.
Q3. i) Calculate the change in GPE. ii) The energy has moved from the GPE to the KE store.
Q4. Will the temperature be closer to ice or the cold drink?
Q5. The line starting nearer room temperature is less steep.
Q6. i)-ii) What else does the fire heat apart from the potato? iii) Compare how much energy is wasted by each.

Hints

Gravity

4.1 Gravity & distance
Q2. How does gravitational force vary with distance?
Q3. How do Jupiter and Saturn compare with other planets?
Q4. At 2, is the rock closer to Earth or the Moon?

4.2 Seasons & daylight
Q2. Which season is it? Does it receive more or less energy?
Q3. How many daylight hours before and after midday?
Q4. Draw a line to show the path of each position to see how much time they are in sunlight.

4.3 Changing appearance
Q2. Which side of the Moon is bright?
Q3. i)-iv) How much of the bright side of Venus can someone on Earth see? Which side?
Q4. Where can the probe see just a bit of the left side of Io?

4.4 Planetary orbits
Q2. i)-ii) The planet further from the star has a longer orbit and receives less radiation. iii) What does zero tilt mean?
Q3. The planets are icy, so have temperatures below zero.
Q4. Further from the Sun, an object receives less radiation.

4.5 Calculate weight
Q2. Does the weight (on Earth) exceed the breaking force?
Q3. What is the weight of the laptop on Mars?
Q4. Mass is the same on Earth as on the Moon.

4.6 Mixed up problems
Q1. i)-iii) Which planet or the Sun is the probe closest to?
Q2. i)-ii) How much of the day is the location in sunlight?
Q3. Think which half of each Moon will be bright.
Q4. Distance from the Sun affects the length of an orbit.
Q5. Which value do you put in the formula $W = m \times g$?
Q6. i)-ii) Distance to the star affects the orbit and amount of radiation it receives. iii) Tilt causes seasons.

Changing substances

5.1 Chemical change evidence
Q2. i)-iii) Is there one of the signs of a new substance?
Q3. i)-iii) Is there one of the signs of a new substance?
Q4. Is there a permanent colour change?

5.2 Physical change evidence
Q2. i)-iv) Are they changes of state, making a mixture or easily reversed?
Q3. i)-iv) Are they changes of state, making a mixture or easily reversed?
Q4. Which experiment looks the same at the end?

5.3 Mass change
Q2. What happened to the mass of copper?
Q3. i) Is there one of the signs of a new substance? ii) Why did the change stop?
Q4. Could this be a physical change?

5.4 Find pH with indicator
Q2. Which indicator shows a colour change around pH 3?
Q3. What is the lowest pH red where onion is dark and the highest pH where tomato is light?
Q4. Which indicator shows a colour change around pH 4?

5.5 Make solutions neutral
Q2. Which side of neutral are the soil samples?
Q3. What do you need to neutralise the sting?
Q4. i)-ii) How does this relate to neutralisation?

5.6 Mixed up problems
Q1. Which observation is a sign of chemical change?
Q2. What are the bubbles likely to be?
Q3. i)-ii) Is there one of the signs of a new substance?
Q4. i) How could the tablets reduce acidity? ii) Why does the stomach need to be acidic?
Q5. Do you need red or blue paper or both?
Q6. Do leaves change at all during the year?

Substances & particles

6.1 Identify dyes
Q2. What does the distance moved by the spots tell you?
Q3. All three contain the spots for tomato.
Q4. Why does the distance moved by the solvent matter?

6.2 Separate two substances
Q2. i)-ii) What different properties do the substances have?
Q3. i)-ii) What different properties do the substances have?
Q4. i) Filtering removes particles which cannot pass through a filter ii) Do water and salt have low boiling points?

6.3 Explain state changes
Q2. What happens to particle energy when the heater is on?
Q3. What happens to particle energy when solid->liquid?
Q4. What happens to the particles in melting and boiling?

6.4 Changing states
Q2. i)-iii) Is the temperature above/below the melting and boiling points?
Q3. Is the temperature above/below melting/boiling points?
Q4. Which have a different range from melting to boiling?

6.5 Solubility data
Q2. i) At what temperature would 30 g fit into the table? ii) 50 g of water is half of 100 g.
Q3. i) At what temperature would 40 g fit into the table? ii) 1 litre of water has a mass 10 times 100 g.
Q4. If he added more than 24 g, some would not dissolve.

6.6 Solubility curves
Q2. Remember to draw a curved line of best fit.
Q3. i)-ii) How much dissolves at the two temperatures?
Q4. i) Where do the lines have the same value? ii) What is the lowest temperature 50 g dissolves?

6.7 Mixed up problems.
Q1. How do the spots in the sample compare to the dyes?
Q2. Flavour/alcohol have a lower boiling point than water.
Q3. The air transfers energy to the particles in the puddle.
Q4. i) Look at the temperatures for no salt/salt. ii) What state is water with rock salt in? iii) Which type is still liquid?
Q5. Compare the values as fractions e.g. A is 10 g / 40 g.
Q6. Make sure you follow the right curve.

Hints

Cells

7.1 Functions of cell parts
Q2. A full vacuole pushes against the cell wall.
Q3. Ribosomes make proteins to help chemical reactions.
Q4. Energy for the cell is released from food in mitochondria.
7.2 Using a microscope
Q2. Mitochondria are tiny structures found inside cells.
Q3. Compare image with the microscope in question 1.
Q4. How do you calculate total magnification?
7.3 Identify cells
Q2. Which labelled features are from plant/animal cells?
Q3. Which labelled features are from plant cells?
Q4. Identify what parts each cell has.
7.4 Functions of specialised cells
Q2. The cell can change shape - where might this be useful?
Q3. It has a very thick cell wall - what is its function?
Q4. Why might skin need no gaps between its cells?
7.5 How cells are specialised
Q2. A blood cell changes shape when it meets a bacteria cell.
Q3. Cilia can help to move particles on the cell's surface.
Q4. How are the cells walls between phloem cells special?
7.6 Mixed up problems
Q1. What does each labelled cell part do?
Q2. What is the magnification of the objective lens he uses?
Q3. What part from animal and plant cells is missing?
Q4. What happens to stoma when guard cells change shape?
Q5. How do white blood cells move to the microorganisms?
Q6. Energy is needed for growth.

Interdependence

8.1 Interpret food webs
Q2. Which organism stores the energy from the Sun?
Q3. The manure is decaying.
Q4. Draw a food chain for a human being.
8.2 Change in population
Q2. What do both snails and slugs eat?
Q3. What do both squid and fish eat?
Q4. Mountain lions eat a greater variety of food than hawks.
8.3 Explain resources
Q2. What happens if plants get more water and warmth.
Q3. What resources affect the growth of plants?
Q4. What resources for survival are scarce in the desert?
8.4 Effect on population
Q2. How could the tree affect the population of daisies?
Q3. Why do butterflies and caterpillars need plants?
Q4. The lines show the population of both animals increases.
8.5 Explain competition
Q2. What do both soy plants and weeds need to grow?
Q3. What do the cheetahs need to survive?
Q4. What happens to the numbers of stoats?
8.6 Mixed up problems
Q1. Grass is a producer.
Q2. Work out what animals kites, snakes and owls eat.
Q3. Minerals are a resource that plants need.
Q4. The population of both animals decreases over time.
Q5. What does fewer plants mean for rhododendrons?
Q6. How does the heavy metal get into the food chain?

Reproduction

9.1 Sexual vs asexual
Q2. This is an example of sexual reproduction.
Q3. There is one parent: what type of reproduction is it?
Q4. The gametes are egg and sperm: who donated these?
9.2 Human reproductive organs
Q2. Where does fertilisation take place?
Q3. One sperm has to meet the egg. It's a difficult journey.
Q4. How can cilia and mucus help the egg travel?
9.3 Menstrual cycle
Q2. What is the function of the uterus lining?
Q3. Is day 18 before or after ovulation?
Q4. What is happening to the uterus lining on day 24?
9.4 Pregnancy time
Q2. After ovulation, an egg only survives for 1 day.
Q3. What happens at the same time the temperature rises?
Q4. Ovulation happens on day 14.
9.5 Supporting the foetus
Q2. Instead of one placenta for a foetus, twins have to share.
Q3. What does the mother's blood supply the foetus with?
Q4. What is the function of the umbilical cord?
9.6 Mixed up problems
Q1. How many parents are involved?
Q2. The sperm needs a tail to swim.
Q3. What happens to the uterus lining during menstruation?
Q4. The events don't always happen as in the diagram.
Q5. The foetus gets less oxygen if its mother smokes.
Q6. Which stage is asexual reproduction and which sexual?

Answers

Contact forces

1.1 Find missing forces
Q2. 2000 N.
Q3. 100 N.
Q4. 15 N.

1.2 Explain floating & sinking
Q2. The boat floats higher as it is less dense.
Q3. i) it will sink. ii) It will float.
Q4. The balloon sinks.

1.3 Calculate density
Q2. A.
Q3. 18 g/cm3.
Q4. A.

1.4 Friction factors
Q2. Missing values: 2, 2.4 N. 3, 3.6 N. 4, 4.8 N.
Q3. A.
Q4. The different weights or different surfaces of the shoes.

1.5 Friction and motion
Q2. i) From 0-10 s the forward force is much bigger than air resistance. ii) The forces are balanced.
Q3. i) The speed increases quickly then more slowly. ii) From 0-2 s the weight is much larger than the drag. After this the net force decreases.
Q4. i) Air resistance increases and becomes as big as the weight.
ii)

1.6 Mixed up problems
Q1. 25 N.
Q2. C.
Q3. D.
Q4. ii)

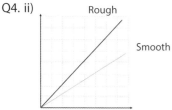

Q5. C
Q6. i) A. ii) C.

Electric circuits

2.1 Complete loops
Q2. Open switch D and close switch E.
Q3. No, they are both on or both off.
Q4. Two bulbs.

2.2 Ammeter readings
Q2. 0.7 A.
Q3. i) 0.4 A. ii) The reading will decrease.
Q4. A.

2.3 Bulb brightness
Q2. Circuit 1.
Q3. C.
Q4. C.

2.4 Batteries to bulbs
Q2. E, A, C, B, D (off).
Q3. i) A circuit with more batteries than bulbs. ii) A circuit with the same number of batteries and bulbs. Iii) A circuit with more than one bulb per battery but less than two bulbs per battery.
Q4. A circuit with 6 bulbs.

2.5 Mixed up problems
Q1. The switch can be anywhere between the battery and where the loops split.
Q2. 2.3 A.
Q3. Bulb P will still be bright and Q still dim.
Q4. i) C. ii) D. iii) A and B.
Q5. i) Switch Z also turns off bulb C. ii) A circuit with switch Z on the middle wire either side of bulb B.
Q6. A2.

Answers

Energy transfer

3.1 Identify energy change
Q2. D.
Q3.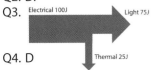
Q4. D

3.2 Energy in/out
Q2. 67.5 minutes (2024 kJ /30 kJ/min).
Q3. i) Two servings = 1800 kJ.
   ii) 300 minutes (5 hours).
Q4. 300 kJ. The sum is 1800 kJ - (30 x 30) kJ– (40 x 15) kJ.

3.3 KE and GPE transfers
Q2. i) 0.25 J. ii) Just before the end - 0.5 J.
Q3. i) Just before it hits the ground - E. ii) A. iii) C.
Q4. i) A. ii) Just above the ground - C. iii) D. iv) B.

3.4 Temperature change
Q2. 50 °C.
Q3. 40 °C.
Q4. 100 g.

3.5 Temperature graphs
Q2. C.
Q3.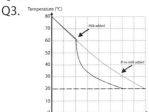
Q4.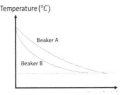

3.6 Interpret energy diagrams
Q2. i) 100 J (5 squares from 10). ii) 20 J (1 square from 10).
Q3. At the top - C
Q4. C

3.7 Identify wasted energy
Q2. i) input: chemical, output: light, sound, heat (thermal). ii) useful: light, sound, wasted: heat.
Q3. i) Friction in motor/pulley. ii) Electrical -> kinetic & gravitational potential stores.
Q4. As car goes down, some energy is lost as heat and sound. On the next hill there is less in the gravitational store, so it can only climb a lower hill.

3.8 Calculate efficiency
Q2. i) Engine A (efficiency is 1/4 or 0.25). ii) Engine A: KE = 100kJ (0.25 x 400). Engine B: KE = 240kJ (0.6 x 400).
Q3. ¼ or 0.25.
Q4. 1/10 or 0.1.

3.9 Mixed up problems
Q1. C
Q2. i) 50 g (for 700 kJ). ii) 30 minutes.
Q3. i) 100 J. ii) 400 J.
Q4. D.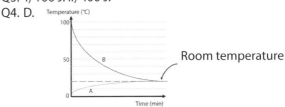
Q5.
Q6. i) Chemical -> potato (thermal, useful) and air/ground (thermal, wasted). ii) Less energy wasted. iii) Fire heats potato/ground/air. Oven heats only potato and air.

Gravity

4.1 Gravity & distance
Q2. 2, 1, 3.
Q3. i) Path goes around Uranus anti-clockwise. ii) Jupiter/ Saturn have greater mass and larger gravity to move comet.
Q4. A.

4.2 Seasons & daylight
Q2.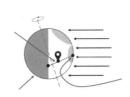
Q3. Pi
Q4. Panel receives less energy at Y.

4.3 Changing appearance
Q2. i) C. ii) B. iii) D. iv) A.
Q3. i) D. ii) C. iii) A. iv) B.
Q4. A.

4.4 Planetary orbits
Q2. i) d has a longer year length. ii) d has a lower temperature. iii) Neither planet has seasons.
Q3. Pluto: year length 248, temperature -218 °C. Eris: year length 560, temperature -240 °C.
Q4. A diagram (like Q1): energy or rays fan out from Sun with fewer hitting distant places.

4.5 Calculate weight
Q2. No, the weight on Earth = 1000 N.
Q3. No, the weight on Mars = 10 N.
Q4. Yes, the weight = 360 N.

4.6 Mixed up problems
Q1. i) Earth. ii) Sun. iii) Jupiter.
Q2. i), Winter, B. ii), Summer, A.
Q3. C.
Q4. Year length.
Q5. 184 N.
Q6. i) a) K-186f has a shorter year than Earth. ii)) Its surface temperature could be higher than the Earth's because it is closer to its star. iii K-186f has no tilt so its days do not vary.

Answers

Changing substances

5.1 Chemical change evidence
Q2. i) Chemical change. ii) No chemical change. iii) Chemical change.
Q3. i) Chemical change. ii) No chemical change. iii) Maybe a chemical change.
Q4. No, it was a physical change.

5.2 Physical change evidence
Q2. i) and iv).
Q3. ii) and iv).
Q4. Experiment B.

5.3 Mass change
Q2. There was a chemical reaction.
Q3. i) The fizzing, and mass decreased. ii) One reactant was used up.
Q4. Janine was wrong.

5.4 Find pH with indicator
Q2. Peach skin
Q3. pH 5.5-9.5.
Q4. i) pH is 6 or below. ii) Methyl orange.

5.5 Make solutions neutral
Q2. i) An acid to neutralise the soil. ii) Louis' soil needs more acid.
Q3. i) Bicarbonate of soda. ii) Vinegar. iii) Bicarbonate of soda.
Q4. i) An Alkali. ii) Check when the colour goes green.

5.6 Mixed up problems
Q1. Jamie, because the reaction gives out light (Or Adi, with the reason that it could just be glowing).
Q2. No. The bubbles are likely to be water vapour coming out of solution.
Q3. i) Colour change and mass decrease. ii) No change as all the copper had reacted.
Q4. i) It contains alkali to neutralise some of the acid. ii) The stomach may not be acidic enough to kill bacteria.
Q5. Red paper staying red and blue paper staying blue.
Q6. We see leaves permanently change colour in the autumn.

Substances & particles

6.1 Identify dyes
Q2. Suspects B and C.
Q3.

Q4. Madder, as the dye moved 9/10 the distance of the solvent.

6.2 Separate two substances
Q2. i) Filtering. ii) Evaporating.
Q3. i) Filtering. ii) Separating funnel.
Q4. i) The salt is dissolved in water. ii) Distillation.

6.3 Explain state changes
Q2. Water particles gained energy and escaped the forces of attraction, and water turns to vapour.
Q3. Water particles in ice gain energy, and partly overcome the forces of attraction, and ice turns to liquid.
Q4. Experiment 2, because particles escape as the water boils.

6.4 Changing states
Q2. i) Solid. ii) Liquid. iii) Gas.
Q3. Bromine: Liquid. Chlorine: Gas. Iodine: Solid. Acetaldehyde: Solid. Formaldehyde: Gas.
Q4. C and D.

6.5 Solubility data
Q2. i) B. ii) 12 g.
Q3. i) B. ii) 700 g.
Q4. 9 g.

6.6 Solubility curves
Q2. An answer between 15-17 g.
Q3. i) An answer between 38-42 g. ii) An answer between 8-12 g.
Q4 i) An answer between 53-57 g. ii) An answer between 41-45 °C.

6.7 Mixed up problems
Q1. Ruth, because the spots moved the same distance as both dyes.
Q2. i) Flavour substances and alcohol have a lower boiling point than water. ii) Distillation.
Q3. Warmer air transfers more energy to the water particles, which overcome the forces of attraction and escape from the liquid.
Q4. i) Lowers the freezing temperature. ii) It freezes. iii) Magnesium chloride.
Q5. D.
Q6. i) An answer between 76-79 g. ii) An answer between 72-75 °C. iii) An answer between 18-20 °C.

Answers

Cells

7.1 Functions of cell parts
Q2. There is not enough water in the vacuole. The empty vacuole cannot push against the cell wall. The cell collapses.
Q3. If ribosomes are destroyed, the bacteria cannot make proteins and cannot carry out chemical reactions to keep it alive.
Q4. The more mitochondria a cell has, the more energy it releases. Muscle cells need energy for movement.

7.2 Using a microscope
Q2. Choose an objective lens with a higher magnification. This increases the total magnification to see smaller structures.
Q3. The mirror is pointing in the wrong direction. Move the mirror so light reflects up through the slide.
Q4. The total magnification is 40 X, not 4 X.

7.3 Identify cells
Q2. It is a plant cell because it has chloroplasts and vacuoles. Animal cells do not have these parts.
Q3. It is an animal cell (nerve cell or neurone). It has a cell membrane and nucleus but no features of a plant cell, e.g. cell wall or chloroplasts.
Q4. A and C could be plant cells. They have a nucleus and a cell wall outside the cell membrane. Cell walls only appear in plant cells.

7.4 Functions of specialised cells
Q2. B - muscle cell. The cell can change its length. Muscles do this to cause movement.
Q3. B - to form the outer covering of seeds. The thick cell makes a sclerid cell strong and tough, to protect seeds before they germinate.
Q4. The cells act as a barrier between outside and inside the body. They are tightly packed so there are no gaps. This prevents microorganisms from entering.

7.5 How cells are specialised
Q2. White blood cell change shape and 'eat' (destroy) the bacterial cell.
Q3. The cilia move back and forth to remove any particles and microorganisms in the airways from the lungs.
Q4. The cell walls between the phloem cells contain tiny holes to allow sap to pass through.

7.6 Mixed up problems
Q1. The chloroplast. Photosynthesis takes place in chloroplasts.
Q2. C (10 x 5 = 50).
Q3. This cell does not have a nucleus. It is a bacterial cell. Its DNA floats in the cytoplasm. In plant and animal cells, DNA is found inside a nucleus.
Q4. The guard cells control the opening and closing of the stoma.
Q5. White blood cells change shape to squeeze through gaps in the walls of the blood vessels. This lets them travel to whereever microorganisms are.
Q6. Some of his mitochondria are not working and not releasing energy from food. Building new tissue for growth requires energy, so Pryesh is less able to grow.

Interdependence

8.1 Interpret food webs
Q2. Producers store energy from sunlight. When eaten, energy moves to the snail, which is eaten by the frog.
Q3. Manure is animal waste, and stores energy. Decomposers decay the manure and release energy as heat.
Q4. Plants are producers, storing energy. It moves to animals (and humans) who store it in cells and tissues.

8.2 Change in population
Q2. More snails reduces the number of dandelions. Slugs eat dandelions so this means fewer slugs.
Q3. Squid and fish eat krill. Fewer fish means more krill for the squid, so their numbers could increase.
Q4. Fewer shrews means lions have 3 organisms to eat. Hawks rely on squirrels and might not get enough.

8.3 Explain resources
Q2. Plants get more water, warmth and light. This means more food for mice, and then more food for owls.
Q3. Ring A is thicker so the tree grew more. This might be due to more rain, warmth, light or minerals.
Q4. Cacti need water and there isn't much in the desert. Plants need long roots to get as much as they can.

8.4 Effect on population
Q2. The number of daisy plants was lower near the tree. It blocks light and reduces the number of plants.
Q3. Butterflies have fewer places to lay eggs, which means fewer caterpillars, and butterflies).
Q4. The number of rabbits increases, then the number of foxes. More rabbits means more food for foxes.

8.5 Explain competition
Q2. Soy and weeds compete for water and minerals. Removing weeds gives soy access to more resources.
Q3. Cheetahs eat deer. The faster the cheetah the more deer it will catch and increases its survival chances.
Q4. There were more weasels with fewer stoats to compete with. Then with more stoats, competition grew.

8.6 Mixed up problems
Q1. Grass stores energy. When eaten, energy moves to the rabbit. The owl eats the rabbit and gains its energy.
Q2. i) Kites only eat snakes so fewer snakes means fewer kites. ii) Owls and snakes eat mice. Fewer snakes means more mice and more food for owls.
Q3. Fertilisers add minerals to soil. Plants can make more proteins and grow better. The farmer earns more.
Q4. The number of hawks dropped, most in 2006. This is because of fewer mice and so less food.
Q5. Rhododendron compete for water, light and minerals. Their poison kills other plants, reducing competition.
Q6. Heavy metals pass up the food chain from phytoplankton, to the fish and eventually to humans.

Answers

Reproduction

9.1 Sexual vs asexual
Q2. It was sexual reproduction. Genetic material from the ovule combined with material from the pollen.
Q3. i) All have identical characteristics. ii) B and C were from asexual reproduction from parent A.
Q4. Kerry and Tom. The baby will have half Kerry's genetic material and half Tom's.

9.2 Human reproductive organs
Q2. An egg is released but stopped by the blockage. It prevent the sperm meeting the egg and fertilising it.
Q3. So many sperm are released to increase the chance that at least one will find the egg and fertilise it.
Q4. The egg sticks to the mucus. The cilia sweep the mucus and egg along the oviduct away from the ovary.

9.3 Menstrual cycle
Q2. The lining gets thicker. It needs to be thick so a fertilised egg can settle into it and grow into a foetus.
Q3. Y: just after ovulation.
Q4. B.

9.4 Pregnancy time
Q2. The earliest date on a live egg and sperm could meet is the 21st. The latest is the 26th.
Q3. The woman should have sex either on the same day as the temperature rise or on the day after.
Q4. The egg will die on day 15/16 so fertilisation will not take place even if sexual intercourse occurs.

9.5 Supporting the foetus
Q2. Twins share oxygen/food and get half that of a single pregnancy. They make fewer new cells and grow less.
Q3. A foetus needs food/oxygen to make new cells. It gets these from mother's blood so her heart pumps more.
Q4. Squashing the cord means squashing blood vessels and so less blood will be reaching the baby.

9.6 Mixed up problems
Q1. Asexual reproduction because there is only one parent, and the offspring look identical to the parent.
Q2. Sperm with shorter tails do not swim as well. If all are like this then, it is likely none will reach the egg.
Q3. C. This is when the lining of the uterus thins as it breaks down.
Q4. A woman can ovulate at any point in the cycle. For some women this can change from month to month
Q5. The foetus gets less oxygen because the mother's blood is carrying less oxygen. Growth slows.
Q6. Stage 1 is asexual, creating copies. Then one joins with a different alga and genetic material combines.

Watch out

10.1 Contact forces
Q2. C.

10.2 Electric circuits
Q2. A, B, E.

10.3 Energy transfer
Q2. D. Energy moves from kinetic to gravitational potential store.

10.4 Gravity
Q2. D. Weight depends on gravity.

10.5 Chemical change
Q2. Physical change. No new substance is made. Adding beetroot juice only makes a mixture.

10.6 Substances & particles
Q2. 200 g (100 g dissolves in 100 g of water).

10.7 Cells
Q2. B. It isn't an animal cell because it has a cell wall. It isn't a plant cell because it doesn't have a nucleus.

10.8 Interdependence
Q2. It decreases. Less grain means mice and grasshoppers eat less. Their numbers drop, meaning less food for owls.

10.9 Reproduction
Q2. Menstruation should start on18th of February as it begins approximately 7 days after ovulation (day 21).

Acknowledgements

Mastery Science Practice Book 1   First published 2017   ISBN 9780956681041

Text copyright Mastery Science Ltd. Design by Alexandra Okada, Stuart Norwood. Images by Gemma Young.

The publisher would like to thank the following for permission to reproduce photographs:

p46 Map data: Google. p87 Microscope: Wiki commons. p89 Sclereid cell: Wiki commons
Images from the Noun Project: p13 Skydiver: Cullen Mertens. p32 Thermometer: Adrien Coquet.
p42 Skydiver: Gan Khoon Lay. p44 Comet: Maxim Samos. p45 Uranus: lastspark. p44 Sun: ruliani.
p54 Probe: Victor Korobkov. p54 Jupiter: Kevin White. p80 Puddle: Bakunetsu Kaito. p80 Eye:
yasminvisible. p102 Chair: Katelyn Maxon. p102 Organism: Mohamad Sabbagh p106 Embryo:
Eugene Khvan p106. People: Gan Khoon Lay.

All remaining images copyright free stock from Shutterstock.